Diversity an[d]

Unit 1

Diversity and Inclusion

1.0 PreK

OVERVIEW

Unit 1 focuses on engaging children with one another in order to discover shared characteristics, experiences, and interests, to explore how each person is unique, to build a sense of community within the classroom, and to recognize how each child contributes to and is valued by this community.

GOALS

This unit is designed to help children:
- Get to know one another.
- Develop comfort in interacting with unfamiliar peers.
- Discover and appreciate commonalities.
- Appreciate and learn from diversity.
- Develop an attitude of inclusion.
- Embrace a shared classroom identity.
- Feel valued as an individual and as a member of the group.

ACTIVITIES

1.1 Getting to Know Each Other
Children discuss the value of getting to know all of their classmates, and play a game in which they share about themselves with their peers.

1.2 Discovering Commonalities
Children discuss how talking and spending time with their peers can help them find things in common with one another, and then have an opportunity to find things that they have in common with a buddy.

1.3 Learning from Diversity
Children discuss how everyone is different in some ways and that this makes each person unique and interesting, and how diversity allows everyone to learn with and from one another.

1.4 Building Community
Children discuss what it means to belong to a community, and then work together to create a representation of their classroom community.

Home-School Connections — Unit 1 (PreK)

1.1 Getting to Know Each Other

Suggested information to share with families in the classroom newsletter:

Our class is talking about what it means to be a friend and why it is important to get to know all of our classmates, and we are playing games that give everyone a chance to share about themselves and learn about each other.

You may wish to:

- Ask your child if they greeted anyone when they got to school today, and what they said.
- Ask your child if they played with anyone new today, and what they did together.

1.2 Discovering Commonalities

Suggested information to share with families in the classroom newsletter:

Our class is talking about the many things that we might have in common with one another, and how some things on the outside are easy to see, but we have to get to know each other better so we can discover some of the ways that we are the same on the inside.

You may wish to:

Have a conversation with your child about ways that your family members are similar or different. For example, compare whether (and how much) each of you do or don't like the following activities, and why.

Cleaning your room *Eating (chose a food)*
Taking a walk *Reading a book*
Going to bed *Riding a bike*

Home-School Connections — Unit 1 (PreK)

1.3 Learning from Diversity

Suggested information to share with families in the classroom newsletter:

Our class is talking about the many ways that each person in our class has unique characteristics and strengths, and how we can learn and try many new things with one another.

You may wish to:

- Ask your child what diversity means.
- Ask your child what is something that they are good at doing or that makes them proud
- Ask your child what is something new that they learned or tried at school this week, and if they did it with someone else.

1.4 Building Community

Suggested information to share with families in the classroom newsletter:

Our class is talking about what it means to belong to a community and how community members treat and work with one another.

You may wish to:

- Ask your child what it means to *belong*.
- Ask your child what it means to be a *community*.
- Talk with your child about some of the communities or groups to which your family belongs.

Getting To Know Each Other

1.1 PreK

OVERVIEW

Read and Discuss: *Meet Z*

Explore and Practice: Get to Know You Ball

MATERIALS

- *Meet Z* storybook
- Ball

GOALS

This set of activities is designed to:
- Emphasize the value of peer relationships.
- Promote the importance of getting to know one another.
- Motivate children to engage with *all* of their peers.

LEARNING OBJECTIVES

Children will be able to:
- Share information about themselves with the class.
- Recall information they have learned about their peers.

KEY CONCEPTS AND VOCABULARY

Friends are important!

Getting to know one another helps us understand each other and get along.

Getting To Know Each Other

1.1 PreK

RESEARCH AND RELEVANCE

Beginnings are important. The start of a new school year is a time for children to rekindle prior friendships, meet new people, and become familiar with the everyday activities and routines of the classroom. Taking time at the beginning of the year to make sure that children are introduced (and introduce themselves) to each and every one of their classmates can help them become engaged and gain comfort with all of their peers. This establishes a norm that *all* children in the class are important to one another, which can lay the foundation for relationships and learning to grow.

Think about this…

Do unfamiliar social situations make you feel excited, comfortable, or anxious?

How do you typically approach new people?

Are there certain kinds of children in your classroom that are easier or more challenging for you to get to know?

Try this today…

Today (and every day), try to make a personal connection with as many children in your classroom as possible—greet a child individually and ask him what he is looking forward to that day, notice what a child is doing and ask her a specific question about it, or remember and follow-up on something a child shared earlier.

Getting To Know Each Other

1.1 PreK

READ AND DISCUSS: MEET Z

Children listen to the story and discuss what it means to be a friend and what it is like to get to know someone new.

Before Reading

Have you ever met a new friend? What do you like about having friends?

In this story, some kids just like you meet a new friend—a very special alien named Z. Z isn't a he or a she—just a Z! The kids decide to help Z learn about children on earth and about friendship!

As you listen to this story, pay attention to what the characters say and how they feel when they meet new friends.

During Reading

Z didn't know what a friend was. What would you tell Z? *(Someone you play with, someone you like to spend time with, someone you get along with)*

How did the kids and Z feel when they met one another? *(Happy, excited, nervous)* **How do you feel when you meet someone new?**

When Z got to the tree house, all the kids greeted Z. To *greet* **someone means to say hello or introduce yourself. How do you think that made Z feel?** *(Happy, welcomed, comfortable)*

After Reading

What is something you could say to a new friend at school? *(Hi, my name is_____, do you want to play?)*

What are some things that you can do with friends at school? *(Talk, play games, ride bikes, read books)*

Extension: Have children turn to their buddy and practice saying a greeting (e.g., *hi, hello, good morning*) in a friendly voice or waving hello.

sanfordharmonyprogram.org ©Arizona State University All Rights Reserved

Getting To Know Each Other

1.1 — PreK

EXPLORE AND PRACTICE: GET TO KNOW YOU BALL

Children share information about themselves as they pass around a ball.

Set the Stage

Gather children into a circle and share something interesting about yourself (e.g., a pet or hobby) that they are unlikely to know. Allow the class to ask 1-2 questions about your share, and then ask children if they learned something new about you. Discuss why it is important for everyone in the class to learn more about one another.

We want everyone in our class to feel welcomed and to feel good about being together. Getting to know one another is important because it helps us understand each other better and get along. We're going to be doing a lot of things together so we can really get to know each and every person in our class.

Facilitate the Activity

Explain that in this activity, everyone will have a chance to get to know one another better by sharing something about themselves with the class, and listening to what their classmates share. Roll a ball to a child and ask them a question (e.g., *Jaden, what is your favorite animal?*). After the child answers, instruct her to pass the ball to a classmate, addressing the peer by name and asking the same question. Continue this process with several children, and then announce a new question to be asked before continuing again.

Tip: Have children clasp their hands in their laps after answering, so that children know to pass the ball to a different peer for a turn.

Suggested Get-to-Know-You Questions
- *What is something that you like to play outside?*
- *What is your favorite book?*
- *What is your favorite belonging?*
- *What is your favorite dessert?*
- *What is a game that you like to play?*

Wrap it Up

How did you feel when your classmates listened to you share about yourself? *(Happy, important, good)*

What is something new that you learned about a classmate today?

Extension: Have buddies pair up and pass a ball back and forth as they answer get-to-know-you questions that you announce.

Getting To Know Each Other

1.1 PreK

SUPPLEMENTAL ACTIVITIES

Me and Z: Invite one or two children each week to bring home a Z figure and a *Me and Z* family letter, instructing them to keep Z with them as they go about the things that they normally do at home. Families might choose to help their child draw, write, or photograph the things that Z "learned" about their child and family. After children return Z and their Me and Z letter to school, invite them to share their experiences with the class and guide classmates in asking questions about the share.

You may wish to **1)** send home the *Get to Know Me* activity sheet for families to help their child complete (with words, drawings, or photos) and return, or **2)** cut a copy of the sheet into 6 cards (setting aside the name and age sections) for use during the activity.

Learning about My Buddy: At the end of the week, invite children to draw and/or dictate something new that they learned about their buddy (e.g., provide a prompt if necessary, such as something my buddy likes, something my buddy likes to do).

Personal Treasure Days: Ahead of time, ask families to help their child choose a small item that has special meaning to them—a personal "treasure"—and have children bring the item (or a photo, drawing, or short description of it) to share with the class. With the whole group (perhaps across several days), invite children to share about their treasures one at a time and allow time for a few questions from classmates. Extend the idea by holding "Personal Treasure Days" at different times throughout the year, suggesting particular types of items at various times (e.g., *Bring a favorite item from your bedroom ~ Wear your favorite t-shirt ~ Bring a special item from a family holiday celebration ~ Bring your favorite book*).

Share Your Square: Lay carpet squares or hand towels in a circle on the floor, with one square for each buddy pair. Play music or sing, and have children march around or dance in the middle of the circle. When the music stops, children should stand on a square (two children will have to share a square). Announce a get-to-know-you question and have children tell their answer to the person sharing their square. Repeat with additional rounds as time allows.

Me and Z

PreK

We want to help everyone in our class to learn more about each other, so your child will be bringing Z home this week. Some things that your child could help Z "learn" might be about your family members, pets, favorite meals or books, or things that your child loves to do at home.

In the space below, your child can draw, attach photos, or you might help write a note about some of the things that Z learns about your child. Please return this, along with Z, next week so that your child can share with the class and help everyone learn more about all of the things that make your child special!

Discovering Commonalities

1.2 PreK

OVERVIEW

Read and Discuss: *Finding Things in Common*

Explore and Practice: How Are We the Same Hunt

MATERIALS

- *Finding Things in Common* storybook
- Bucket or container (one per buddy pair; optional)

GOALS

This set of activities is designed to:
- Promote an awareness of commonalities with others.
- Encourage comfort in sharing about oneself.
- Foster openness toward learning about others.

LEARNING OBJECTIVES

Children will be able to:
- Identify things they have in common with peers.

KEY CONCEPTS AND VOCABULARY

Having things *in common* means that there are things that are the same about you both.

Getting to know one another helps you discover things that you have in common.

Discovering Commonalities

1.2 PreK

RESEARCH AND RELEVANCE

Spending time with someone new or less familiar is not always easy. It feels good to have things in common with friends, and children are often more motivated to play with and befriend others who seem to be "like them"—and may feel less comfortable to interact with those who seem "different" from them. Sometimes decisions about whether another child is similar to oneself are based on simple—and often visual—cues of similarity, such as gender or race. Helping children to discover what they might have in common with each of their classmates can help them feel a sense of connection with one another and can provide new, shared foundations for conversations and play. This can encourage children to talk and play with a wider range of their peers, broadening their social and learning experiences.

Think about this…

In thinking about your own close relationships, what qualities do you feel are important or are you attracted to in others? Are these similar, different, and/or complementary to your own characteristics?

What are some benefits of having friends with whom you share things in common?

What kinds of similarities or differences do you think are most important or most prevalent in children's close friendships—interests, temperaments, gender, social skills, other qualities?

Try this today…

Find opportunities to draw children's attention to what they may have in common with their classmates. When children discuss interests, feelings, or experiences, take a moment to ask if others share that preference, have felt that way, or have been in a similar situation. Occasionally, ask the whole class and graph the responses (emphasizing that all responses are valued, not just the most frequent or popular response).

Discovering Commonalities

1.2 PreK

READ AND DISCUSS: *FINDING THINGS IN COMMON*

Children listen to the story and discuss how talking and getting to know others can help you discover commonalities—even with those who may seem very different.

Before Reading

Have you ever played with someone that you didn't know very well? How did you feel? What did you do together?

In this story, Z feels nervous about playing with new friends, and doesn't know what they can do together. The kids help Z learn that even if someone seems new or different, you can discover things that you have *in common*—things that are the same about both of you.

As you listen to the story, pay attention to what the characters have in common, or ways they are the same.

During Reading

How did Z feel when seeing the new kids? *(Nervous, scared, shy)* How could you tell? *(Acted shy, stayed across the room, whispered)*

Why do you think Z felt that way? *(Z was new, didn't know the kids very well, didn't know what they liked to play, felt different)*

If Mia didn't ask Z what Z liked to do, would they have found out that they all liked playing the same game? Why is it important to talk and try to get to know each other? *(You can learn things that you don't know; you can find things that you have in common)*

After Reading

Z was worried that the kids wouldn't like Z and wouldn't want to play because they were different. Did that happen? What happened instead? *(They talked to each other, found things they all liked, found things they had in common, had fun playing together)*

If you wanted to play with someone new, what could you do to find out what you both would like to play? *(Talk to them, ask them what they like to do)*

Extension: Have children turn to their buddy and practice asking what they like to play (e.g., *What do you like to play outside?*), and compare if their answers are different or the same.

Discovering Commonalities

1.2

EXPLORE AND PRACTICE: HOW ARE WE THE SAME HUNT

Children practice identifying things they have in common with classmates, and then search in the classroom for interests they share with their buddies.

Set the Stage

Gather children into a circle. Review what it means to have something *in common* (you are the same or similar in that way), providing a few examples (e.g., *Jack and Annie both have on red shirts—wearing red shirts is something they have in common.*).

Next, ask a question about children's characteristics (e.g., *Who has a pet at home?*) and have them step into the middle of the circle if it is true of them. Point out to the class that the children in the circle have something *in common* and are the same in that way. Have children rejoin the circle and then repeat with additional questions.

Tip: Ask about **skills** (*knows how to swim*), **preferences** (*likes to watch funny movies*), **experiences** (*has been to a baseball game*), and **personal history** (*has a sister*). Be sensitive in choosing questions so that children do not feel singled out.

Facilitate the Activity

Explain that children will be playing a game to discover some of the things they have in common with their buddies. Give each buddy pair a container to hold items from the hunt. Set a time limit, and instruct each buddy pair to hunt in the classroom and find two items that they <u>both</u> like to play with or do at school. Remind buddies that they must talk to one another to make sure that the items are things that they <u>both</u> enjoy.

After the hunt, gather children together and invite them to share what they have in common.

Wrap it Up

What did you and your buddy discover that you have in common?

What did you learn about your buddy that you didn't know before?

Extension: Allow buddies to play together with their selections for a designated time.

Discovering Commonalities

1.2

SUPPLEMENTAL ACTIVITIES

Similarities Simon Says: Play a version of Simon Says in which children are to follow movement commands only if they have a given characteristic (e.g., *Simon Says if you have pet, put your finger on your nose*). During the game, have the class look around at their classmates to notice which children share those characteristics in common, and ask follow-up questions or give additional commands (e.g., *All of the children standing on one leg have pets. Simon Says if your pet is a dog, start hopping on one leg*). End the game and have children sit down together in one group by giving a command that uses a characteristic shared by all (e.g., *have a birthday, live in Arizona, have ever felt happy*).

What We Like Collages: Using pictures in old magazines, have buddies create a collage of things that they both like.

Learning from Diversity

1.3 PreK

OVERVIEW

Read and Discuss: *Celebrating Diversity*

Explore and Practice: Being Different Is Awesome

GOALS

This set of activities is designed to:
- Encourage an appreciation of diversity.
- Foster openness toward learning about and from others.
- Promote respect for others.
- Foster a sense of being valued as an individual.

LEARNING OBJECTIVES

Children will be able to:
- Name reasons why diversity is beneficial.

KEY CONCEPTS AND VOCABULARY

Diversity means that everyone is a little bit different, and no one is exactly the same.

Diversity makes everyone unique and interesting.

You can learn new things from each other.

Having *respect* for someone means that you think good things about them and treat them kindly.

MATERIALS
- *Celebrating Diversity* storybook
- *What If* cards

Learning from Diversity

1.3 PreK

RESEARCH AND RELEVANCE

Each person brings to their interactions and relationships a unique set of experiences, interests, abilities, heritage, and temperamental qualities. Sometimes children can find these differences interesting, but sometimes they may view these differences as...*very different* from them. Respecting and appreciating what makes each person unique can foster understanding, empathy, and positive attitudes toward others. These skills will support children's ability to live in a diverse world and to have friendships and relationships with all kinds of people. They will also learn that it's okay to be different in some ways, and that those differences (in themselves and others) are accepted and valued. Everyone can learn from diversity!

Think about this...

What kinds of people do you tend to befriend first at your workplace, in your neighborhood, or at social gatherings?

In your classroom, do you find yourself drawn more to children with certain kinds of characteristics than to others? Are these similar, different, and/or complementary to your own characteristics?

What are some benefits of having friends with whom you differ (e.g., differ in ability, age, race, gender, life history, etc.)?

Try this today...

Take advantage of opportunities when you can direct children toward a peer to provide information or assistance, emphasizing their particular knowledge, experiences, or skills.

That was a great book we just read about reptiles. I know that you have a pet lizard at home, Max—could we ask you some questions about what it's like to take care of a reptile?

Learning from Diversity

1.3 PreK

READ AND DISCUSS: CELEBRATING DIVERSITY

Children listen to the story and discuss diversity, respect, and how you can learn new things from others who are different from you in some ways.

Before Reading

Has anyone ever taught you how to do something new that you had never tried before? What did you learn that was new and different?

In this story, Z doesn't understand why one of the kids likes to do something that is different than what Z likes. The kids help Z learn that it's okay for friends to be different. *Diversity* means that everyone is a little bit different, and no one is exactly the same. Because everyone is different, you can learn about a lot of new and interesting things from each other.

As you listen to the story, pay attention for a time when Z learns something new from a friend who likes something different from Z.

During Reading

Why did Z think that Kenny should stop working in the garden? *(Gardening was different than what Z liked, Z thought gardening looked boring, Z had never tried gardening)*

How would Kenny have felt if he had to stop gardening like Z said? *(Sad, he would miss gardening)*

What did Z learn from Kenny at the end of the story? *(How to take care of the plant, how to work in the garden)* If Z hadn't been willing to try something new with Kenny and learn about plants, what could have happened? *(The plant could have died, Kenny's feelings could have been hurt, Z wouldn't have learned something new)*

After Reading

Having *respect* for someone means that you think good things about them and that you treat them kindly. Is it important to show respect to everyone, even if they do things differently from you? How can you show respect to someone who does things differently? *(Listen to them, be polite, say kind things to them)*

Learning from Diversity

1.3 PreK

Can you still get along and play with someone if you each like different things? How can you do that? *(Learn about what each other likes, try playing something new together, find something that you both have in common)*

Extension: Have children turn and tell their buddies something that they like to play, and compare to see if they like the same or different things.

EXPLORE AND PRACTICE: BEING DIFFERENT IS AWESOME

Children predict what it would be like if everything was exactly the same, and discuss the value of diversity.

Set the Stage

Ask a question (e.g., *What do you like to eat for dinner? What do you like to play outside?*) and choose a child to respond. Next, invite several children to share a *different* answer, pointing out how many diverse answers children have.

People can be the same or different in many ways—in how they look or how they feel or what they like to do. Diversity means that everyone is a little bit different, and that's what makes each one of us interesting and unique!

Facilitate the Activity

Explain that the class will be imagining what it would be like if there was no diversity and everyone and everything was the same. Invite a volunteer to choose a *What If* card, then read the scenario and challenge children to imagine doing the same thing, in the same way, all the time. (e.g., *Who likes to play ball? What if we ONLY played with balls on the playground this year? Balls would be the only things on the playground, and we would all play with balls every single day, every time we went outside. What would that be like?)*

Brainstorm the pros and cons of the situation, and have the class vote (thumbs up/down) whether they would want it to be the same all the time. Emphasize the benefits of having diversity (e.g., *Isn't it AWESOME that we have a lot of different choices in what to do on the playground?*). Repeat with additional *What If* scenarios.

Discuss how differences allow people to learn new things with and from one another.

Learning from Diversity

1.3 PreK

It's fun to discover things we have in common, but if everyone was *exactly* the same – looked the same, sounded same, did the same things – things would get pretty boring. Diversity makes our class and the world a more interesting place, and because we are all different, we can learn and do a lot of new things with one another.

Wrap it Up

What would it be like if everyone in our class was exactly the same? *(Boring, not very much fun, would never get to do anything new)*

What is good about having and playing with lots of different classmates? *(You can try new things, you can learn about each other, you could be the same or different in many ways)*

SUPPLEMENTAL ACTIVITIES

Diversity Displays: Choose a topic (e.g., something they like to play, what their bed looks like) for children to illustrate. As a group, compare children's illustrations and discuss similarities and differences. Create a display of children's work and emphasize how it shows all of their diversity.

What Makes Me Proud: Gather children into a circle and have them think of something that makes them feel good about themselves or feel proud (provide examples). Go around the circle and invite children to share with the class. After every few children, invite them into the center of the circle to dance or wave pom-pom-poms as the class chants a "hooray" cheer for them.

What We Like Collages: Provide paper (one piece per buddy pair) and old magazines, and have buddies find and cut pictures to glue onto a collage of things that they like. Encourage children to talk to one another to find out what things they like that are different or the same.

What if…	What if…
 You had to play with the same kind of toy every day	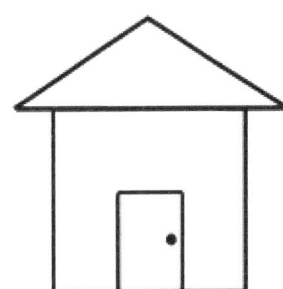 You lived in the same kind of house as everyone else
What if…	What if…
 There was only one flavor of ice cream	 You could only play with the same person every day
What if…	What if…
 You had to eat the same lunch every day	 Everything was the same color

1.3 What If Cards (PreK)

Building Community

1.4 PreK

OVERVIEW

Read and Discuss: *Belonging Together*

Explore and Practice: Our Classroom Community

GOALS

This set of activities is designed to:
- Promote a sense of connection and community within the classroom.
- Foster a feeling of being valued and accepted as a member of the group.
- Encourage social responsibility toward the classroom community and its members.

LEARNING OBJECTIVES

Children will be able to:
- Reflect on what it means to be a community.
- Identify their classroom as a community.
- Work cooperatively to create a representation of their classroom community.

KEY CONCEPTS AND VOCABULARY

A *community* is a group of people who have something in common or do things with one another.

When you *belong*, you are a part of a group with other people.

Everyone in the class belongs to the classroom community.

MATERIALS

- *Belonging Together* storybook
- Butcher paper and art supplies
- Photos of children (optional)

If you have not already done so, consider a name to establish for your classroom community (e.g., the Shining Stars, the Room B3 Kids, etc.).

Building Community

1.4 PreK

RESEARCH AND RELEVANCE

Children learn and grow best when they have a sense of belonging and feel welcome, accepted, and connected to others in their lives. Although children can belong to many different groups, emphasizing the classroom community as an important part of their social identity highlights the shared connection that they have with each and every one of their classmates. This nurtures an awareness of others (*all* others) and a sense of responsibility and caring toward each of their classmates. When the classroom community joins in celebrating the uniqueness of each individual child as well as the qualities and accomplishments of the group, children can develop their sense of being *me* while also learning to be a part of *we*.

Think about this…

To what groups or communities do you belong?

Do you feel that you have a sense of comfort and connection within these groups? How does having or not having this sense impact your interpersonal or work experiences within these groups?

Try this today…

Use positive reinforcement to build a sense of connection and community responsibility by pointing out how children's actions can benefit the group, using the classroom name when possible.

All our Panda Bears really worked together to clean up the outside toys very quickly! Now we will all have time to hear an extra story together before lunch.

Maria, it was really kind of you to give some of the markers to Jeremy. Sharing with each other helps everyone have a chance to draw.

Building Community

1.4 PreK

READ AND DISCUSS: BELONGING TOGETHER

Children listen to the story and discuss what it means to belong to a community, and how they all belong to the classroom community.

Before Reading

People can be a part of many different kinds of groups, like a family or a team or a community. What are some groups that you belong to?

In this story, Z worries that it might be time to leave the tree house and the kids. The kids help Z understand that Z belongs with them. When you *belong*, you are a part of a group with other people. Everyone who belongs is important to one another.

As you listen to the story, pay attention to how Z feels about belonging together with the kids.

Tip: Provide examples and ask children to raise their hand if they belong to that group, making sure to include their class as a group to which they all belong.

During Reading

Z didn't understand about *belonging* and thought it was time to leave the tree house. How would you explain to Z what it means to belong? *(To be a part of a group, to be together with others, to be part of a community)*

Why did Z feel happy to belong with the kids at the tree house? *(Z liked the kids, Z felt like they cared about Z, Z liked to be at the tree house)*

After Reading

A community is a group of people who have something in common or do things with one another. When you are part of a community, how do you think you should treat one another? *(Do things together, care about one another, respect one another)*

What do we do together that makes our class a community? *(Learn and play together, care about each other, eat together, take care of the classroom together)*

Extension: Have children turn to "someone in their classroom community" and give them a high-five.

Building Community

1.4 — PreK

EXPLORE AND PRACTICE: OUR CLASSROOM COMMUNITY

Children discuss what makes their classroom a community, and then work cooperatively to create a representation of their classroom community.

Set the Stage

Ask children to raise their hand if they belong to the *(class name)* community. Have children look around at their classmates and remind them that everyone that belongs is an important part of the community. Invite children to share some things that they like about being part of their class community (e.g., *What's great about being a [class name]?*).

Facilitate the Activity

Explain that children will be creating a representation of their classroom community together.

Today we are going to make something together that shows that we all belong to the *(class name)*. **We will keep it in our classroom so that we can see it every day, and it will help us remember that we all belong to our classroom community. Everyone will work on it together because we all are an important part of our class.**

Have children work together to make a banner or other representation of the classroom community (add photos if desired). Encourage cooperation by having children share materials or work with buddies or in small groups to work on different aspects of the project. (If working on a common paper, state the expectation that no one will cover another person's work).

Add the class name to the banner and have children help decide where to display it in the classroom. Gather children together to discuss the experience.

Variation: Have buddies trace or paint each other's hands on one large banner.

Wrap it Up

Why was it important for everyone to work on this together? *(Everyone is part of the class; everyone cooperates and does things together)*

What are some ways that we worked together like a community to make this? *(Helped each other, shared things, cooperated)*

Building Community

1.4 PreK

How do you feel when you look at what our class made together? *(Happy, like we belong, proud, included)*

Tip: Frequently using the class name can reinforce the common identity children share and foster a sense of connection with classmates (e.g., *Okay, Busy Bees, it's time to come to the circle!*).

SUPPLEMENTAL ACTIVITIES

Classroom Community Helper Pledges: Have children write/draw what they can do that week to help the classroom community.

Hooray Song: Choose an energetic song or chant and sing it together as a whole group. During each round of the song, choose one or more children to dance in the middle of the circle or shake pom-poms, while the rest of the class sings, claps, and cheers for them. End the song by calling the classroom name and having everyone stand to dance and cheer for the whole class.

Our Many Communities: Using magazine pictures or photographs gathered from families, show children images of different types of groups or communities and invite them to guess what they are, and then discuss what they have in common (e.g., people working together).

Pass around pictures: Give each child in a small group a piece of paper. Have children draw for a short time and then rotate the paper to the next child in the group until all children have drawn on all of the papers. Display the drawings together and emphasize how they were made together.

Z Sing-Along CD: Have a class discussion about activities that are more fun or successful to do with a friend or a group (rather than alone), and then sing and dance to *We're Better Together*.

Empathy and Critical Thinking

Unit 2

Empathy and Critical Thinking

2.0 PreK

OVERVIEW

Unit 2 focuses on promoting emotion understanding and empathy and helping children become flexible thinkers by becoming aware and thinking critically about their own ideas and about the messages they receive from others.

GOALS

This unit is designed to help children:

- Develop emotion understanding, including recognizing feelings and identifying their causes and consequences
- Develop empathy for others
- Increase flexible thinking and decrease stereotyped thinking
- Develop incremental (change) thinking

ACTIVITIES

2.1 Recognizing Feelings
Children learn to identify and demonstrate the physical signs of different emotions.
Children discuss how various emotions look, sound, and feel, and then practice demonstrating different emotions in a game.

2.2 Predicting Feelings
Children discuss how to think ahead and predict emotions that might result from a given situation, and then practice predicting how they might feel in different situations.

2.3 Explaining Feelings
Children discuss how you can think back to what happened first or looking for situational cues in order to understand reasons for someone's feelings, and brainstorm reasons that people can have different feelings.

2.4 Having Empathy
Children discuss what it means to have empathy for someone, and sing about ways to show empathy and caring to someone in different situations.

2.5 Understanding Stereotypes about People
Children discuss how not everyone in a group is just the same, and practice a way to respond to stereotypes, emphasizing that "some do, some don't."

2.6 Understanding Stereotypes about Objects, Activities, and Roles
Children discuss how everyone can make choices and that toys, activities, and roles can be for everyone, and practice a way to respond to stereotypes.

2.7 Understanding that People Can Change
Children discuss the potential for growth, learning, and change in themselves and others and identify how they have changed.

Home-School Connections — Unit 2 (PreK)

2.1 Recognizing Feelings

Suggested information to share with families in the classroom newsletter:

Our class is learning about different emotions and how they can change the way your body looks and sounds on the outside and feels on the inside.

You may wish to:

- Play *Feelings Charades* with your child, taking turns guessing the emotion that the other person is demonstrating or describing. Use your whole body and/or tone of voice to demonstrate the emotion, or describe the physical sensations that you might experience.
- Use a variety of emotion words to help your child name how they are feeling and to describe how their body feels inside (e.g., stomach in knots, hot cheeks, butterflies in the stomach).
- Play music and dance as if you are feeling a certain emotion, then switch to another emotion. Or, play different types of music (e.g., upbeat, slow tempo) and as your child how it makes them feel.

2.2 Predicting Feelings

Suggested information to share with families in the classroom newsletter:

Our class is learning that emotions are one way that we react to things and situations, and that you can *think ahead* in order to try and predict, or guess, how someone might feel after something happens.

You may wish to:

- While reading books together, pause after story events occur and invite your child to *think ahead* and predict how the character might feel next.
- Talk with your child about ways that people react emotionally to different situations. For example, discuss how each of you (or other family members) would feel in scenarios such as the following scenarios, and why your feelings might be the same or different.
    - You are about to take off the runway in an airplane.
    - You have nothing to do for the next hour.
    - You just finished a really hard puzzle.
    - A neighbor's dog comes over and licks you.
    - Someone tells you that you did a great job.

Home-School Connections — Unit 2 PreK

2.3 Explaining Feelings

Suggested information to share with families in the classroom newsletter:

Our class is learning that in order to understand someone's feelings, you can look for clues in the situation or you can *think back* to what happened first.

You may wish to:

- Ask your child what it means to be a *feelings detective*.
- While reading books together, pause after the characters express feelings and invite children to *think back* about what events or thoughts might explain why they have those feelings.
- Help your child notice clues about why someone feels a certain way by pointing them out explicitly (e.g., *That child's parent is helping him down from the top of the tall slide. Why do you think he might be crying?*).

2.4 Having Empathy

Suggested information to share with families in the classroom newsletter:

Our class is learning about what it means to understand and feel what someone else is feeling—to have *empathy* for them—and how that can help us show kindness, generosity, and caring toward others.

You may wish to:

- Model empathy by showing an awareness and understanding of your child's feelings—even if you don't share or agree with them (e.g., *I can see that you're angry that you need to stop playing now, but it's time to clean up and get ready for bed.*).
- Explain your own feelings (both positive and negative) to your child to help them understand how others feel and why (e.g., *It makes me so happy when I see you being kind to your sister by sharing your cover with her.*).
- Talk with your child about the consequences of his or her actions (both positive and negative) for others (e.g., *How do you think your friend felt when you said that she couldn't come to your birthday party? That probably hurt her feelings and made her feel very left out.*).

Home-School Connections — Unit 2 PreK

2.5 Understanding Stereotypes about People

Suggested information to share with families in the classroom newsletter:

Our class is talking about having stereotypes—or thinking that everyone in a group is just the same. We are talking about how people can be the same or different in many ways, and that you can only know what each person is really like by talking and spending time together. We are learning to be flexible thinkers and to watch out for words like *all*, *none*, and *only*.

You may wish to:

- Ask your child what it means to have a stereotype.
- Ask your child what they would say to someone who said that ALL kids (or grandparents or teenagers or…) (fill in the blank: *eat cereal for breakfast, like to watch movies, etc*).
- Ask your child what they can do instead of making guesses about what someone is like.

2.6 Understanding Stereotypes about Objects Activities, and Roles

Suggested information to share with families in the classroom newsletter:

Our class is learning that emotions are one way that we react to things and situations, and that you can *think ahead* in order to try and predict, or guess, how someone might feel after something happens.

You may wish to:

- While reading books together, pause after story events occur and invite your child to *think ahead* and predict how the character might feel next.
- Talk with your child about ways that people react emotionally to different situations. For example, discuss how each of you (or other family members) would feel in scenarios such as the following scenarios, and why your feelings might be the same or different.
  - You are about to take off the runway in an airplane.
  - You have nothing to do for the next hour.
  - You just finished a really hard puzzle.
  - A neighbor's dog comes over and licks you.
  - Someone tells you that you did a great job.

Home-School Connections

Unit 2 — PreK

2.7 Understanding That People Can Change

Suggested information to share with families in the classroom newsletter:

Our class is talking about how everyone can change, and that means that we will have lots of opportunities to grow and to learn and to try new things.

You may wish to:

- Ask your child one way they have changed this year.
- Focus on "process rather than product"—praise your child for their efforts rather than what they accomplished (e.g., *I see that you are really working hard at trying to tie your own shoe!*).

Recognizing Feelings

2.1 PreK

OVERVIEW

Read and Discuss: *Feelings on the Outside, Feelings on the Inside*

Explore and Practice: *The Feeling Train*

GOALS

This set of activities is designed to:
- Foster awareness that emotions have internal and external cues.
- Promote recognition of own and others' emotions

LEARNING OBJECTIVES

Children will be able to:
- Describe and demonstrate how basic emotions feel (internal physical sensations) and look and sound (external physical and verbal cues).
- Identify basic emotions based on physical and verbal cues.

KEY CONCEPTS AND VOCABULARY

Emotions, or feelings, can change the way our bodies:
- Look and sound on the outside.
- Feel on the inside.

People can feel and show their emotions differently.

MATERIALS
- *Feelings on the Outside, Feelings on the Inside* storybook
- Whiteboard
- *Emotion Cues* chart (teacher reference)

Recognizing Feelings

2.1

RESEARCH AND RELEVANCE

Emotional development includes children's experience, expression, and regulation of their own emotions, as well as the ability to understand others' emotions and develop empathy. A foundational skill is the ability to identify and label a range of emotions in oneself and others based on internal and external physical cues. Being able to accurately recognize emotions in themselves and others can help children manage their own emotions and interact more competently with others.

Think about this...

How do you physically experience different feelings? Do you tend to have low or high intensity reactions, or does this differ according to feeling?

Are there any types of feelings that are especially familiar or particularly uncomfortable for you to experience?

Try this today...

Help children develop an awareness of their own emotional reactions. When children are experiencing an emotion, help them use descriptive feeling words or refer to feeling pictures displayed in the classroom to identify what is happening with their body on the outside or how their body feels on the inside (making sure that children are not too upset and that it is an appropriate time to discuss feelings).

Recognizing Feelings

2.1

READ AND DISCUSS: FEELINGS ON THE OUTSIDE, FEELINGS ON THE INSIDE.

Children listen to the story and discuss how emotions can change how you look and sound on the outside and how you feel on the inside.

Before Reading

How are you feeling right now—happy, sad, excited, tired?

In this story, Z doesn't know what it means to have feelings, like being happy or sad or afraid. The kids help Z learn that everyone has feelings, or *emotions*, and that they can change how you look and sound on the outside and how you feel on the inside.

As you listen to this story, pay attention to the different emotions that Z and the kids have, and how those feelings change the way they look and sound on the outside and feel on the inside.

During Reading

How did Z feel on the inside when the kids were coming to the tree house? *(Tingly inside, excited)* How could the kids tell that Z was feeling excited to see them? *(Z was smiling, had a cheerful voice)*

How did Jeremy look on the outside when he felt mad? *(Frowns, squeezes his hands and crosses arms)* How did Z feel on the inside when Z was mad? *(Hot and bubbly inside)* How do you look and sound and feel when you are mad?

What did Z want the kids to do when Z felt afraid? *(Wanted the kids to sit close)* What do you do to feel better when you have feelings or emotions that you don't like? *(Think about something happy, talk to someone, hug someone)*

What did Z look like when Z started feeling sad? *(Frowning, looking down)* What did the kids do when they figured out that Z was sad? *(Said that they were coming back tomorrow, helped Z feel better)*

Extension: Have children turn to their buddies and show how they look when they are mad.

After Reading

What are feelings, or emotions? *(How your body looks and sounds on the outside and feels on the inside when something happens)* Does everyone have feelings?

How can you figure out how someone else is feeling? *(Look at their face and body, listen to their voice, ask them how they feel)*

Recognizing Feelings

2.1 PreK

EXPLORE AND PRACTICE: THE FEELING TRAIN

Children describe internal and external emotion cues, and demonstrate different emotions during a movement game.

Set the Stage

Explain that you will be talking about how different emotions, or feelings, change how you look and sound on the outside and how you feel on the inside.

Emotions are feelings, such as happiness or sadness or anger. Emotions can change the way that you feel on the inside of your body. Emotions also can change the way you look and sound on the outside, such as the way your face looks, the way you move your body, or the sound of your voice. Everyone shows their emotions in different ways, but we can pay attention to how someone looks and sounds to try and figure out how they might be feeling.

Demonstrate an emotion using your whole body (refer to the *Emotion Cues* chart), and describe any internal physical sensations that might be experienced with that feeling and the external cues, focusing on different body parts one at a time (e.g., *When I am feeling afraid or scared, I look like this. My eyes open wide and my eyebrows go up like this, and you can see my teeth because my mouth is pulled back. Sometimes I hold my arms in close to my body like this when I'm scared, and my toes curl up, and I feel kind of shaky inside. That makes my voice quivery like you're hearing now.*).

Have children turn to their buddies and demonstrate the emotion, encouraging them to show the feeling with their face and entire body, and to state how they are pretending to feel (e.g., *I'm scared!*), using a voice that matches the feeling.

Tip: Be sensitive to cultural differences in the expression of emotions, and emphasize that everyone shows their emotions in somewhat different ways.

Facilitate the Activity

Explain that children will be playing a game called *The Feeling Train* in which the passengers need to show different emotions in order to come aboard the train.

Have the class stand up in a circle. As the train "conductor", name and demonstrate an emotion with your face, body, and voice, and ask children to describe how you look and sound. Have children turn to their buddy and demonstrate that emotion and then, using an appropriate emotional tone, invite them onto the train behind you (e.g., *Okay, passengers, all aboard the Happy Train!*). Walk around the room (or in a circle) and have children follow you as everyone continues to demonstrate the emotion. Point out how the passengers are showing their feeling (e.g., *We are all on the Sad Train so we are walking so slowly and droopily!*).

Tip: Provide a prompt (e.g., *Show each other how you might look if you were afraid of a big dog that was barking across the street.*).

sanfordharmonyprogram.org ©Arizona State University All Rights Reserved

Recognizing Feelings　　2.1

"Stop" the train at a "station" and then repeat with an additional emotion demonstration, discussion, and *Feeling Train* as time allows. End with a calm feeling so that you can gather children back into a quiet circle for discussion.

Wrap it Up

How were you feeling inside when you were on the *(Emotion) Train*?

What can you do to help you figure out how someone else is feeling? *(Look at their face and body, listen to their voice, ask them how they feel)*

• •

SUPPLEMENTAL ACTIVITY

Feeling Faces: Have children choose an emotion and illustrate, dictate, and/or write about what they feel, look, and sound like when they experience that emotion.

Feelings Collage: Have children work with buddies and give each pair a large piece of paper that is divided into two or more sections, each labeled with an emotion (face and/or name). Have children look through magazines to find pictures of people who are displaying different feelings, and then sort and glue the pictures onto the different sections of the collage.

Feelings Picture Walk: Have buddies pair up to select an illustrated book. Ask children to look through the books together, finding and discussing examples of feelings. Children might also describe feelings illustrated in their book to their buddy and ask them to guess the emotion.

If You're Happy and You Know It: Lead children in singing and acting out emotion verses of *If You're Happy and You Know It*, choosing actions that reflect the corresponding emotion (e.g., "If you're sad and you know it, make a frown.").

Some Emotion Cues

Emotion	Can look like	Can sound like	Can feel like
Anger	Lowered inner eyebrows Bulging eyes Squinting eyes Tightly-pressed lips Crossed arms Clenched fists Stiff body	Yelling Shouting Stomping	Hot Boiling Bubbling Tight
Fear	Raised eyebrows Opened eyes Opened mouth Pulled back corners of the mouth Limbs pulled into body Shaking body	Shaking voice Quivering voice Whimpering	Dry mouth Tight Stiff Sweating Racing heart
Happiness	Raised corners of the mouth Crinkled eyes	Clapping Cheerful voice Squealing Laughing	Bubbling Jumping Relaxed
Sadness	Raised inner eyebrows Lowered eyelids Lowered corners of the mouth Trembling lip Slumped, drooping body	Crying Sobbing Moaning Whining	Weak Weepy Droopy
Surprise	Arched eyebrows Widely-opened eyes Dropped jaw Palms raised Sudden backward movement	Gasping Screaming Cheering	Racing heart Jumpy

2.1 Emotion Cues (PreK)

How would you feel if…

you were at the top of a tall slide?

How would you feel if…

you saw a big dog?

How would you feel if…

you dropped your ice cream cone?

How would you feel if…

someone said something mean to you?

How would you feel if…

someone asked you to play?

How would you feel if…

it was your birthday?

2.1 How Would You Feel? (PreK)

sanfordharmonyprogram.org ©Arizona State University All Rights Reserved

Predicting Feelings

2.2 PreK

OVERVIEW

Read and Discuss: *Predicting Feelings*

Explore and Practice: Back-to-Back Predictions

GOALS

This set of activities is designed to:
- Increase understanding of emotional consequences of situations.
- Foster awareness that people can feel different emotions about the same situation.

LEARNING OBJECTIVES

Children will be able to:
- Predict emotions based on situational cues.

KEY CONCEPTS AND VOCABULARY

One way you react to things that happen is with your feelings.

To *predict* means to make a guess about what might happen next.

You can *think ahead* and try to predict how someone might feel after something happens.

People can have different feelings about the same situation.

MATERIALS

- *Predicting Feelings* storybook
- *How Would You Feel* scenario cards

Predicting Feelings

2.2

RESEARCH AND RELEVANCE

Social-emotional learning includes emotion understanding skills such as the ability to predict what feelings would likely result from a particular experience, and the recognition that people can have different thoughts and feelings about the same situation. Understanding this variability in cognitive and emotional reactions allows children to begin to understand the perspectives of others, an important relationship skill.

Think about this...

Do you find that it is easier to predict the feelings of some adults or children than others? Does that impact the way you interact with those people in any way?

Have you ever been in a situation in which your emotional response differed greatly from someone else's who was involved in the same situation? What was that like for you?

Try this today...

While reading books aloud, pause after story events occur and invite children to predict how the character might feel next. If characters react in a surprising way, discuss why.

Predicting Feelings

2.2 PreK

READ AND DISCUSS: PREDICTING

Children listen to the story and discuss how you can think about what is happening in order to guess or predict how someone might be feeling.

Before Reading

If you saw someone get hurt, how would you guess they might be feeling after that? How would you guess that someone might feel after they got a fun birthday present?

In this story, the kids help Z learn how to predict people's feelings, or how to guess how people might feel after different things happen. Thinking about how someone might be feeling can help you understand them and get along.

As you listen to the story, pay attention for times when Z or the kids predict or make a guess about how someone else is feeling.

Tip: Show children the cover illustration and invite them to "predict" or guess what the story might about.

During Reading

How would you predict or guess that Annie might feel when she learns that the clay is dry and hard? *(Sad, disappointed, angry)* Why do you think she would feel that way? *(She really wanted to play with the clay)*

How would you predict or guess that Annie might feel when she finds out there is another bucket of clay? *(Happy, glad, excited)*

How do you think Gabriel was feeling while his clay snakes kept breaking? *(Frustrated, mad, disappointed)* What did Annie and Z do to find out for sure how Gabriel was feeling? *(Asked how he felt)*

Why did Z think that Gabriel would be afraid of Annie's clay bug? *(Z was scared so Z thought Gabriel would be scared too)* Was Z's prediction right? Why did Z guess wrong? *(Gabriel thought that bugs were cool, people can feel differently about the same thing)*

Tip: As different situations occur, have children think about how the characters might be feeling before continuing the story to find out.

After Reading

What does it mean to *predict* how someone feels? *(Guess how they feel, think about what is going on so you can figure out how they feel)*

Why is it okay to feel differently about the same thing? *(Everyone is different; people can have different ideas and feelings)*

sanfordharmonyprogram.org ©Arizona State University All Rights Reserved

Predicting Feelings

2.2

EXPLORE AND PRACTICE: BACK-TO-BACK PREDICTIONS

Children predict how they might feel in various situations.

Set the Stage

Choose a situation likely to elicit a strong emotional reaction in children, and ask them to imagine how they would feel in that situation (e.g., *How would you feel if a fire truck was going to visit our school today?*). Invite a few children to share their reactions, and ask if anyone would have a different feeling, emphasizing that sometimes people feel differently about the same thing. Summarize how the situation would make the class feel (e.g., *So if a fire truck came to our school, most of you would be really excited and a couple of you would feel a little nervous.*).

Facilitate the Activity

Describe how to predict someone's feelings based on the situation that has happened.

When things happen, one way you react to them is with your feelings. Different situations might make you feel happy or angry or scared or sad. When you know what is happening, you can try to *predict* how someone might feel next. To *predict* means to *think ahead and guess* how someone might feel after something happens.

Explain that children will be playing a game to practice predicting how they might feel when different things happen, and to see if they would feel the same way as their buddy.

Choose a *How Would You Feel* scenario and guide two buddy volunteers in modeling a back-to-back prediction. Have buddies stand back-to-back and read the scenario out loud. Ask children to think about whether they would feel happy, sad, angry, or scared if that happened to them, and to make the face that shows that feeling. Count to three and have the children around to see one another's expression.

Have the class stand back-to-back with their buddies and continue the game. Discuss whether buddies would feel the same or differently in various situations, and why.

Wrap it Up

If you know what happened to someone, what might you be able to guess? *(How they feel, what they might do next)*

What can you do to figure out if your prediction or guess is actually how the person feels? *(ask the person, look for clues in how they look and sound)*

sanfordharmonyprogram.org   ©Arizona State University All Rights Reserved

Predicting Feelings

SUPPLEMENTAL ACTIVITIES

Peek-a-Boo Predictions: Read a *How Would You Feel* scenario and have a volunteer silently think of how they would feel. Have the class make predictions and share them quietly with their buddy, and then close their eyes. Ask the volunteer to demonstrate the emotion they would feel in that situation, and then have the class open their eyes to see if their prediction was correct.

Explaining Feelings

2.3 PreK

OVERVIEW

Read and Discuss: *Being a Feelings Detective*

Explore and Practice: Reasons for Feelings

GOALS

This set of activities is designed to:
- Increase understanding of causes of emotions.
- Promote an awareness of behavioral and situational cues in understanding emotions.

LEARNING OBJECTIVES

Children will be able to:
- Identify reasons for emotions based on situational cues.
- Generate reasons for different emotions.

KEY CONCEPTS AND VOCABULARY

There can be many different reasons for someone's feelings.

You can *think back* to what happened first to try and understand how someone is feeling.

You can pay attention to what is happening to find clues about why someone feels the way they do.

MATERIALS

- *Being a Feelings Detective* storybook
- *Reasons for Feelings scenario pictures*
- *Feeling Face cards*

Explaining Feelings

2.3 PreK

RESEARCH AND RELEVANCE

In addition to being able to predict how someone might respond to a situation (feelings as consequences), emotion understanding includes the ability to recognize the situations that may result in a given feeling (causes or explanations of feelings). Children with greater emotion understanding tend to do better in school, both socially and academically.

Think about this…

Have you ever noticed that a child in your classroom seemed to be having a really bad day? What did you say or do? What do you say or do when you see someone who seems to be in a very good mood?

Try this today…

While reading books aloud, pause after characters exhibit emotional reactions and invite children to *think back* to identify events or thoughts that explain why they have those feelings.

Explaining Feelings

2.3

READ AND DISCUSS: BEING A FEELINGS DETECTIVE

Children listen to the story and discuss how to try and understand someone's feelings by looking for clues and thinking back to what happened first.

Before Reading

Have you ever noticed someone looking sad, but weren't sure why? What did you do?

In this story, Z has to figure out why one of the kids is feeling sad. The rest of the kids help Z learn how to be a "feelings detective" by looking for clues and by thinking back about what happened first in order to understand why their friend feels sad.

As you listen to the story, pay attention to what Z has to think about to figure out why one of the children is feeling sad.

During Reading

How do you think Kenny was feeling when he found his friends painting? *(Happy, excited)* Why do you think he was feeling happy? *(He loves to paint; he wanted to paint with his favorite color)*

How do you think Kenny was feeling when he sat down next to the puzzle box? *(Sad, disappointed)* What clues showed that he was sad? *(He sighed, put his head in his hand, didn't play with the puzzle, frowned)*

Thinking back, what happened right before Kenny started looking sad? *(Z said there wouldn't be any purple paint left)* Why do you think Kenny was sad? *(He wasn't going to be able to use the purple paint; Z didn't share the paint with him)*

How was it helpful for Z and the kids to figure out why Kenny was sad? *(They understood how he felt; they were able to do something to help him)*

After Reading

What can you do to figure out why someone feels like they do? *(Ask them, look around for clues, think back to what happened first, guess how someone might feel in that situation)*

Why is it important to try and understand how someone is feeling or why they feel that way? *(To show that you care, so you will know how to respond)*

Explaining Feelings

2.3 PreK

EXPLORE AND PRACTICE: REASONS FOR FEELINGS

Children generate possible reasons for various feelings.

Set the Stage

Show the class the first *Reasons for Feelings* picture and ask how the child is feeling (*angry, mad*) and how they can tell that he feels that way (*frowning, arms crossed, stomping foot*), and then brainstorm possible reasons.

What are some reasons that he might be feeling angry? *(He can't find a toy he wants, he doesn't want to stop playing, someone else has a toy that he wants)*

Next, show the second picture and have children "be a feeling detective" and identify the clue and the reason why the child is angry (*his block tower fell over*). Explain that in order to figure out why someone is feeling a certain way, you can think back to what happened or look for clues about what happened.

People can have a lot of feelings, and there can be many different reasons for the ways that people feel. To figure out *why* someone feels a certain way, you can *think back* to what happened first or you can look for clues about what is going on or what they are doing right then. Figuring out the why someone feels the way they do can help us understand them.

Facilitate the Activity

Explain that the class will be thinking about some of the reasons that people might have different feelings. Invite a volunteer to draw a *Feeling Face* card and identify the feeling. Have the class think of reasons why they might feel that way at school (e.g., *What is something that might make you feel happy when you are at school?*) and share their answers with their buddies. Have the volunteer to share a reason, and, when applicable (when there would be clear clues), ask the class how they might know if someone was feeling that way for that reason (e.g., *How would you know if someone was sad because they fell down—what clues would you see? They would be crying and rubbing their knee, you might see them fall, they might tell you what happened.*). Invite 2-3 other children to share their reasons for that feeling as well, highlighting similarities and differences. Repeat with additional feelings.

Wrap it Up

When we see someone who looks (emotion), what can we do to help us figure out why they are feeling that way? *(Think back to what happened first, look at what is going on for clues, ask them)*

Explaining Feelings

2.3

SUPPLEMENTAL ACTIVITIES

Reasons for My Feelings: Have children choose an emotion and write/dictate and illustrate something that makes them feel that way. Gather children together to share the many reasons for different feelings, highlighting similarities and differences.

2.4 Feeling Face cards (PreK)

Having Empathy

2.4 PreK

OVERVIEW

Read and Discuss: *Knowing Just How Someone Feels*

Explore and Practice: *If Your Buddy's Feeling Happy*

GOALS

This set of activities is designed to:
- Promote understanding of others' perspectives and feelings.
- Promote empathic responding to others' emotions.

LEARNING OBJECTIVES

Children will be able to:
- Describe ways to show empathy and caring to someone in a given situation.

KEY CONCEPTS AND VOCABULARY

Having *empathy* means that you can feel and understand how someone else feels.

Understanding how someone feels can help you be a good friend to them.

MATERIALS
- *Knowing Just How Someone Feels* storybook

Having Empathy

2.4

RESEARCH AND RELEVANCE

Empathy is the ability to identify with and understand another person's emotions—to feel what they feel. To have empathy, children must have some awareness and recognition of their own and other's emotions. In order to act upon empathy and show caring for another's feelings, children must be able to consider those feelings and determine what actions or responses would be appropriate in a given situation. Children with greater empathy behave more pro-socially towards others.

Think about this...

Have you ever experienced being misunderstood because someone did not share or understand your feelings in a given situation?

Have you ever hidden your feelings (e.g., told someonce that you were fine when you actually weren't) because you didn't think they would understand?

What factors can make it hard to respond empathically to someone?

Try this today...

Model empathy for children by showing an awareness and understanding of their feelings—even if you don't share or agree with them (e.g., *I can see that you're all really excited because you just came in from the playground, but it's time to take it easy and get ready to start our next activity.*). Help them understand your feelings as well, both positive and negative (e.g., *It makes me feel very worried when you start running as soon as you go out the door, because someone might trip and get hurt.*).

Having Empathy

2.4 PreK

READ AND DISCUSS: KNOWING JUST HOW SOMEONE FEELS

Children listen to the story and discuss how understanding how someone feels, perhaps because you have felt that way too, can help you figure out how to respond to them in caring ways.

Tip: Show children the cover illustration and invite them to "predict" or guess what the story might about.

Before Reading

Has there ever been a time when you were feeling sad and someone did something nice for you? How did it feel to have someone think about your feelings and be caring towards you?

In this story, Z tries to understand how the kids are feeling, and realizes that sometimes Z has felt that same way too. The kids help Z learn that having *empathy* means feeling and understanding how someone else feels, and that can help you be a good friend to them.

As you listen to the story, pay attention to what Z does when Z knows just how one of the children is feeling.

During Reading

When Kim tripped on a ball and bumped her knee, why did Z think that she might be feeling sad or mad? *(Z thought about how Z felt sad and mad when getting hurt)*

When Z understood just how Kim felt, how did Z show empathy and caring toward her? *(Patted her on the back, picked up the toys so no one else would trip)*

How did Jordan look after his picture was ruined by the paint? *(Sad)* How did Z show empathy and caring for Jordan? *(Z shared the last paper)*

How was bringing Jordan a blanket a good way to show empathy and caring? *(Z thought about how Jordan was feeling tired; Jordan was tired so a blanket was what he needed)*

Tip: As different situations occur, have children think about how the characters might be feeling before continuing the story to find out.

After Reading

When you see someone looking angry or sad, what can you think about to help you understand just how they feel? *(Think about a time when you felt that way, think about what they might want or need)*

How does understanding how other people feel help you be a good friend? *(You will know what to say or do to show that you care, you will understand them better)*

Having Empathy

2.4 PreK

EXPLORE AND PRACTICE: IF YOUR BUDDY IS FEELING

Children sing a song to describe ways to show empathy and caring toward a buddy.

Set the Stage

Have children think of a time when they saw someone who was sad or hurt, and did something kind to show that they cared about them. Invite several children to share what they did and then ask them how they think the person felt afterwards.

Explain that understanding how someone feels can help you figure out how to respond and show caring.

When you have *empathy* and understand how someone else is feeling, you can figure out what to say or do that shows that you care about them.

Facilitate the Activity

Describe or role play an empathy scenario (refer to suggested scenarios below). Have children tell their buddies a way to show empathy and concern to someone in that situation, and then invite one child to share their idea. Lead children in singing a verse of *If Your Buddy's Feeling (Happy)*, using the suggested caring response.

> *If your buddy's feeling happy, give her a high five [clap, clap]*
> *If your buddy's feeling happy, give her a high five [clap, clap]*
> *If your buddy's feeling happy and you want to show you care*
> *If your buddy's feeling happy, give her a high five [clap, clap]*

When applicable, have children turn to their buddies and act out the empathic response. Repeat verses with children's additional ideas for how to show caring, or try a different scenario.

Empathy Scenarios
What could you do if your buddy…
*is **sad** because he fell down?*
is excited because it is her birthday?
is afraid to climb on the jungle gym?
is mad because her tower fell down?
is disappointed that there are no balls left?
is happy because he just finished a puzzle?

Having Empathy 2.4

Wrap it Up

Why is it important to show that we care about how others feel? *(It is kind, it makes them feel good, they know that someone cares about them)*

What could you do if you don't know how someone is feeling or what to do to help them feel better? *(Ask them, ask an adult for help)*

SUPPLEMENTAL ACTIVITIES

How I'm Feeling: Create a set of cards with feeling faces or words (multiples of the same feeling). Keep these in an accessible area and establish a system so that children can use the cards to communicate their feelings to others if they aren't able to do so with words (e.g., they are too upset, they don't know who to talk to). You might encourage children to choose and display cards on their desk or a student chart, or they could hand the card to a friend or an adult. When you introduce the system to children, have a discussion about ways to respond to others' feelings.

Understanding Stereotypes About People

2.5 PreK

OVERVIEW

Read and Discuss: *Some Do, Some Don't*

Explore and Practice: Some Do, Some Don't

MATERIALS

- *Some Do, Some Don't* storybook

GOALS

This set of activities is designed to:
- Foster increased understanding of *variability within* social groups (in preferences, characteristics, and behaviors).
- Foster increased understanding of *similarities across* different social groups (in preferences, characteristics, and behaviors).
- Promote flexible thinking and decrease stereotyped thinking.

LEARNING OBJECTIVES

Children will be able to:
- Describe limitations and problems associated with stereotypes and overgeneralizations.
- Demonstrate ways to challenge stereotypes.

KEY CONCEPTS AND VOCABULARY

Having a *stereotype* means thinking that everyone in a group is just the same.

Stereotypes are just guesses and they aren't always true.

You have to get to know people to know what they are really like.

Overgeneralizing words to avoid: all, every, none, always, never, only.

Some do, some don't.

Some are, some aren't.

Sometimes you do, sometimes you don't.

Understanding Stereotypes About People

2.5 PreK

RESEARCH AND RELEVANCE

Children are natural "sorters"—they tend to group people and things into simple categories in order to make sense of a complex world (everyone does this at times). Social categorization is the grouping of people by an identifiable and meaningful characteristic that is shared in common, such as gender or race.

Advantages of Categorization

- **Organizes** a large body of complex information
- Allows for the use of **inferences** (e.g., can better predict behavior or motives by merely knowing group membership)

Disadvantages of Categorization

But also results in tendencies to:

- View members of the same group as **much more similar** than they actually are
- **Exaggerate differences** between members of different groups
- Use **essentialist thinking,** or the belief that an underlying "essence" (e.g., "boy-ness") exists that ties all members of a group together and makes them similar
- Form **stereotypes** about individuals
- Make **inaccurate assumptions** about individuals based on group membership

Stereotypes are beliefs about individuals based on their membership in a particular social category or group. They are often used to make assumptions about others or to interpret and predict their behavior, and are reflected in overgeneralizations such as *NO boys _____* or *ONLY babies can _____* or *ALL teenagers like_____*. They also send the message that children should think or feel or act a certain way—the same as the others in their "group". Because young children do not yet have highly flexible or sophisticated cognitive skills, it can be challenging to change their stereotypes once they are formed. However, guiding children in thinking critically about the accuracy of these beliefs and messages can help them better understand individual variability within groups and the many similarities across people of different groups.

Understanding Stereotypes About People

2.5 — PreK

Think about this…

Have you ever felt that someone made an assumption about you based on your membership in a particular social category (e.g., age, race, gender, religion, economic class) or community? How did that make you feel?

Have you ever found yourself making assumptions about others based on their social group, before you had a chance to really get to know them? What strategies have you used to avoid doing this?

Have you ever found yourself making overgeneralized statements about the interests, temperaments, or abilities of children who belong to a particular social group? What strategies have you used to avoid doing this?

Do you ever unintentionally draw attention to social categories in your classroom by using social groups to address (e.g., *Good morning boys and girls!*) or organize (e.g., boys' and girls' lines) children? How might this impact children's attitudes about and interactions with one another? Would you use social categories other than gender (e.g., race) to address or organize children in this manner?

Try this today…

Highlighting gender in unnecessary ways can reinforce the notion that gender is a really important way to group (and, thus, separate) people, and that boys are like *X* and girls are like *Y*.

▶ Avoid using gender to organize classroom areas (e.g., seating children boy-girl-boy-girl, boy/girl lines) or activities and routines (e.g., *Let's have the boys wipe off the tables and the girls straighten up the art area. It's the girls' turn in the loft this morning.*)

▶ Also refrain from using gender as a label (e.g., *Line up, boys and girls!* or *The boys in the block area are getting too loud.*) Instead, address children in a way that allows them to focus on their identity as a student and as part of the classroom community (e.g., *Good morning, Panda Bears!* or *The children playing over there with the blocks are getting a little too loud.*)

▶ Try to group and regroup children several times each day based on a random characteristics in order to promote their recognition of the many different groups of which they are all a part.

sanfordharmonyprogram.org ©Arizona State University All Rights Reserved

Understanding Stereotypes About People

2.5 PreK

READ AND DISCUSS: *SOME DO, SOME DON'T*

Children listen to the story and discuss how people can differ in many ways, even though they might have some things in common or may be part of the same group, and identify problems associated with stereotypes and overgeneralizations.

Before Reading

What is something that everyone here has in common, something that is the same about the whole group? Now what is something that might be different about each person here? Even though people are in the same group and have things in common, they can be also be different in many ways too.

In this story, Z thinks that all children are just the same as one another. The kids help Z learn that everyone is different, and that getting to know one other is how you learn what each person is really like.

As you listen to the story, pay attention to what Z thinks about what kids like to play, and if Z's guess is correct or incorrect.

Tip: Class commonalities might include: *have the same classroom, have the same teacher, live in the same city.*

During Reading

Why did Z think that Kim wanted to draw with chalk? *(Z thought she liked the same thing as the other kids)* Was Z right? *(No, she wanted to build sandcastles)*

Having a stereotype means thinking that everyone in the same group is just the same. Did Z have a stereotype about kids? What did Z think about all kids? *(That all kids like to play the same thing)*

Do you think that ALL kids like the same things as one another? *(Some kids do and some kids don't)*

Do you think that kids have to like or do the same things all the time? *(Sometimes kids do and sometimes kids don't)*

After Reading

What can happen when you make a guess about someone instead of asking them what they like or what they like to do? *(You might think the wrong thing, you might not know what they are really like)*

What can you do instead of making guesses about people or thinking that they are the same as other people? *(Talk to them, ask them what they like to do, get to know them)*

Tip: Prompt with examples, but to avoid introducing or reinforcing typical stereotypes (e.g., *Do all girls like pink?*) choose other examples (e.g., *Do all 5-year-olds love the rain?*). When children bring up stereotypes they have heard, address them accordingly.

Understanding Stereotypes About People

2.5

EXPLORE AND PRACTICE: SOME DO, SOME DON'T

Children discuss the problems associated with stereotypes and overgeneralizations, and practice strategies for challenging stereotypes **by emphasizing that "some kids do, some kids don't."**

Set the Stage

Ask a volunteer to share a personal preference or routine (e.g., *What is your favorite breakfast? What time do you go to bed?*). Make the assumption that all children share this in common, exaggerating your reaction (e.g., *Oh, so I guess that ALL of you like cereal the best? You probably ALL eat cereal EVERY SINGLE DAY for breakfast. You sure must like cereal to eat it that much! Maybe we should start eating cereal at school too since you ALL like it so much.*). Give children time to protest (prompt if necessary), and then repeat your claim, pointing out how they are all in the same group (e.g., *But you're all kids/4-year-olds/Busy Bees, so you must ALL like the same breakfast, right?*).

Ask children why they think your assumption isn't true (*kids don't have to like the same thing, Joey likes cereal but Arial likes pancakes, no one is exactly the same, everyone is different*). Summarize the class responses (e.g., *Oh, so even though you are all kids/4-year-olds/Busy Bees, you don't ALL like the same things!*).

Explain the problems associated with overgeneralizations and stereotypes.

When people think that everyone in a group is exactly the same, or likes or does the same things; that is called having a *stereotype*. But stereotypes are just guesses about what people are like, and they are often wrong! You can't know what someone is really like unless you ask them or get to know them.

Facilitate the Activity

Provide examples of overgeneralizations and stereotypes (see below) and guide children in practicing the phrases "some do, some don't" or "some are, some aren't". Divide the circle in half and have children practice the response so that one half of the class chants, for example, "Some kids do" and then the rest of the class responds by chanting "And some kids don't!"

Understanding Stereotypes About People

2.5 PreK

- Give the class an example of a stereotype about a group of people (e.g., boys, girls, teenagers, grandparents, people with brown hair, athletes). **To avoid unintentional reinforcement of stereotypes, do not use "traditional" stereotypes as examples** (i.e., do <u>not</u> choose *boys are good at sports* or *older people can't hear well*.). Rather, use random characteristics (e.g., *I heard someone say that adults don't like bugs.*)

- Ask children if they think the statement is true, and guide them in discussing why it is not (e.g., *What do you think about that? Do you think NO adults like bugs?*), emphasizing that "some do, some don't." Invite children to share counter-stereotypical examples (e.g., *Does anyone know an adult who likes bugs?*)

- State that the statement was a stereotype, and invite children to challenge it (e.g., *What would you say if you heard someone say that adults don't like bugs?*).

- Have the class practice the "some do, some don't" chant (e.g., *Some adults do and some adults don't!*).

Repeat with 2-3 additional examples, guiding children through the process and practicing the chant for each one.

Tip: Add movements by having children [clap, clap, clap] or [stomp, stomp, stomp] as they chant the words.

Wrap it Up

Is it fair to have stereotypes about people and to think they are just like everyone else? What's the problem with thinking that everyone is just the same? *(Stereotypes are just guesses, they could be wrong, everyone is different, no one is exactly the same)*

What should you do instead of guessing what someone else is like or thinking they are just like someone else? *(Ask them, talk to them, spend time with them)*

....

SUPPLEMENTAL ACTIVITIES

Diversity Displays: Choose a topic (e.g., something they like to play, their favorite book) for children to illustrate. As a group, compare children's illustrations and discuss similarities and differences. Create a display of children's work and emphasize how it shows all of the diversity within the class.

Stereotype Catchers: Teach children a hand signal (e.g., palm out in front, showing "stop") to use when they hear a stereotype. Read a story to the class, inserting overgeneralizing statements as you read (*One morning, Suzy went to the library with her mother. <u>They did that because all parents like to go to the library.</u> When they got there…*). When children signal a stereotype (prompt if necessary), stop and have them challenge it, repeating the response for the class (e.g., *Oh, so some parents like the library, and some parents don't.*).

Understanding Stereotypes about Objects, Activities, and Roles

2.6 PreK

OVERVIEW

Read and Discuss: *Things Can Be for Everyone*

Explore and Practice: *Things Can Be for Everyone*

GOALS

This set of activities is designed to:
- Reduce stereotyped thinking about objects, activities, and roles.
- Promote strategies for challenging stereotypes and stereotype-based teasing.
- Promote flexible thinking and decrease stereotyped thinking.

LEARNING OBJECTIVES

Children will be able to:
- Describe limitations and problems associated with stereotypes about objects, activities, and roles.
- Demonstrate ways to challenge stereotypes.

KEY CONCEPTS AND VOCABULARY

Things can be for everyone (as long as it is safe and fair).

It wouldn't be fair if things were only for some people.

MATERIALS

- *Things Can Be for Everyone* storybook
- Object, activity, and role props (e.g., toys, apparel, pictures)

Understanding Stereotypes about Objects, Activities, and Roles

2.6 PreK

RESEARCH AND RELEVANCE

Children are quick to recognize recurrent associations between things (e.g., *Long hair is for moms, but not dads.*), and they form explanations, expectations, and predictions based on this information. Often, these associations reflect their continual observations of the world (e.g., *Mom drives the car when she is by herself, but when she is with Dad, he always drives.*) as well as the many direct and indirect messages they receive about what is appropriate for males and what is appropriate for females—how they should look, dress, and act, what they are like, and what they should do (e.g., *I see only boys in the toy commercials that are loud and flashy.*). These repeated "associations" are the foundations for gender schema—cognitive representations of what it means to be male or female—and are the source of stereotypes. (Cognitive schema form in the same way about other social categories.).

Once stereotypes are formed, young children can be very rigid in applying them to people and things in their world. In fact, as early as preschool some children begin to act as "gender police"—enforcing gender-based stereotypes about toys, clothing, and roles within the classroom. These messages are limiting for children and can make them feel uncomfortable or ashamed of their own individual interests and preferences. Kids often claim to like or dislike things based on whether they think they are "for" their own gender—regardless of whether or not they actually choose to play with these things.

Pink is for girls—you can't wear that.
We're playing knights and warriors. If you want to play with us, you can be the princess we have to save.
Girls are supposed to wear dresses. Why don't you ever wear dresses?
You look like a boy.

Encouraging children's engagement in a variety of activities and roles—including those traditionally gender-typed for their own as well as the other sex—will support the development of a broad range of interests and skills that can increase successful learning. This doesn't mean that children should avoid things that are "stereotyped" for their own sex if they enjoy those activities. It also doesn't mean that every child *should* like or do everything…but they should feel that they *can* if they want.

Understanding Stereotypes about Objects, Activities, and Roles

2.6   PreK

Think about this…

What influenced your engagement in different activities as a child, or now as an adult? What factors impacted your eventual career?

Do you or have you ever crossed typical "gender norms" in your chosen hobbies or social activities? How does that feel? What kind of response have you received from others? Have you ever been reluctant or been discouraged to engage in activities that cross "gender norms"?

Try this today…

Be mindful of the subtle messages that children receive about what is appropriate or not appropriate for their gender.

Describe gender-typed activities and occupations with similarly positive terms to demonstrate that they are equally valued.

- ► Encourage children's involvement in all types of activities, based on their personal preferences, strengths, or areas where they can learn and grow.
- ► Refrain from inviting or assigning children classroom jobs based on gender.
- ► Review classroom literature, posters, and other materials for gender messaging.

Set clear classroom expectations about stereotyping and teasing, and do not allow these behaviors based on gender or any other social category (or, for any reason).

It's not okay to say that Max looks like a girl because he is wearing the crown. Crowns are for everyone, and everyone gets to choose for themselves what they want to wear or play.

Understanding Stereotypes about Objects, Activities, and Roles

2.6 PreK

READ AND DISCUSS: *THINGS CAN BE FOR EVERYONE*

Children discuss fairness and the idea that different toys, activities, and roles can be for everyone.

Before Reading

What are some things that you really like to play? How would you feel if someone told you that those things were just for other kids and not for you?

In this story, Z wonders who can play with certain toys or do certain things. The kids help Z learn that things aren't ONLY for some kids and not for others—that wouldn't be fair, because things can be for everyone!

As you listen to the story, pay attention for what the kids tell Z about who can play with what toys and who can do what activities.

During Reading

When things are <u>fair</u> it means that everyone is treated the same way and that everyone has the chance to do the same kinds of things. Do you think that it would be <u>fair</u> if some toys or activities were only for some of the kids in our class? Who are the toys in our classroom for? *(Everyone)*

What if you really wanted to be a chef or a firefighter or a dancer or a superhero, and someone told you that only some kids could do that, but not you? How would you feel? *(Disappointed, sad, frustrated)* Do you think that would be fair? Who do you think can do those things? *(Everyone)*

Tip: To avoid introducing and reinforcing stereotypes, allow children themselves to bring up any stereotypes that they have encountered, and then address them accordingly.

After Reading

Do you think it is fair for someone to say that only some kids can play with certain toys or do certain activities? What would you say to someone who said that? *(That things can be for everyone, that kids can choose what they like to play, that there are all kinds of kids who like to do those things)*

Are there any things that aren't for all kids? *(Things that are dangerous for kids, things that are someone else's personal belongings)*

Tip: Emphasize how thinking "things can be for everyone" also means that those things must be safe and fair for everyone.

Understanding Stereotypes about Objects, Activities, and Roles

2.6 PreK

EXPLORE AND PRACTICE: THINGS CAN BE FOR EVERYONE

Children identify limitations and problems associated with stereotypes about objects, activities, and roles, and practice strategies for challenging stereotypes.

Set the Stage

Encourage children to consider what it would feel like to be treated unfairly and limited in what they could do. Give kids 1-2 absurd examples and discuss out how silly and unfair they are (avoid using personal characteristics such as gender, hair color, etc. as examples):

Who ate peanut butter and jelly lunch today? What if I said, *Today ONLY the children who had PB&J for lunch will get to play with the bikes. Bikes are just for PB&J kids, so kids who ate something else for lunch can't play with them.*

Now everyone sitting on one of the red carpet squares raise your hand. What if I said, *Today, we're going to have Water Day outside, but if you're sitting on a blue square right now, you can't play. If you're sitting on a blue square, you'll have to play something else.*

For each example, discuss how it would make each group of children (e.g., PB&J versus non-PB&J) feel, and whether it would be fair to everyone.

Tip: Families sometimes express concerns about their child's interests, activities, or friendships, and occasionally these are related to gender-based expectations. Support families by being respectful of cultural values, and focusing on highlighting children's strengths and positive characteristics as you talk with families.

Facilitate the Activity

Explain that it is not fair to say that only some kids can play with certain toys or be certain things.

Sometimes we might hear people say that certain clothes or toys or games or jobs are only for some people and not for others. But that wouldn't be fair. Things can be for everyone, and we each get to make our own choices about how we look and what we like and what we do.

Choose 2-4 play activities, objects (e.g., toys or clothing), or roles (e.g., pretend or real jobs). For each, show children a prop and discuss reasons for wanting to do/have/be those things, who can do so, and how to challenge stereotypes about them, using the example below as a guide.

1) (Show a set of crayons.). **What are these for?** (*Drawing, coloring*) **Why would someone want to draw?** (*like to draw, good at drawing, want to learn how to draw better*)

Tip: Avoid bringing up "typical" stereotypes. If children themselves raise these kinds of stereotypes, address them accordingly. If they are gender-based, remind children that *"there are no boys' things or girls' things— things can be for everyone."*

Understanding Stereotypes about Objects, Activities, and Roles

2.6 PreK

2) Could anyone want to draw? Can children like to draw? Grandparents? Teachers? Kids in the Panda Bears class? *(Yes)* So do you think that drawing is only for some people, or can it be for everyone? *(Everyone)*

3) What if you really liked drawing and someone told you that drawing was just for toddlers. Do you think that would be fair? What could you say to someone who said that? *(Drawing can be for everyone, people can choose what they like to do)*

4) Turn to your buddy and practice saying, *"Drawing can be for everyone!"*

Repeat with several examples, allowing the class to suggest examples as well. If some children insist that stereotypes are true (e.g., *Flowers aren't for everyone—just girls!*), gently guide the class through the process again and help all of the children think about fairness, kindness, and counter-stereotypical examples (e.g., *What if someone in our class really liked flowers and kids told him that he shouldn't have a flower backpack? How do you think he would feel? Would that be fair? Is it okay to hurt people's feelings by saying what they are doing or wearing is wrong? Have you ever seen a boy wearing a flower shirt or backpack with a flower on it?*).

Tip: If children make stereotyped comments, turn the discussion back toward the class with a general example before continuing, in order to avoid singling out or shaming any individual children.

Wrap it Up

How do you know that things in our classroom can be for everyone? *(Everyone can play with everything, you get to choose what to play with)*

- - -

SUPPLEMENTAL ACTIVITIES

Exploring Careers: Throughout the year, invite men and women with a variety of occupations to visit the class and talk about their work. Ideally, invite a male and female with the same occupation to visit at the same time. Ask visitors to share some of the reasons that they chose these careers and why they feel well-suited and/or satisfied with their choices. Use these opportunities as a springboard for new classroom activities or themes that can involve all children.

Someday I'd Like To: Have a class discussion about various activities or occupations, emphasizing that things can be for everyone. Have children illustrate and write about something that they would like to learn or do someday. Gather the class back together to share their work. As children share, ask if any classmates have similar interests.

Understanding Stereotypes about Objects, Activities, and Roles

2.6 PreK

Challenging Stereotypes: Model and then have children practice responses that challenge stereotyped statements, using examples such as the following (you may wish to include a variety of known classroom favorites or points of disagreement):

What if someone said to you…

Who can play with trucks and cars?
> *Everyone!*

Teachers can't play superheroes.
> *That's not true—things can be for everyone, so everyone can play superheroes.*

Who could be the doctor?
> *Everyone!*

The dolls are only for us.
> *Things can be for everyone, and dolls are for everyone if they want to play with them.*

Z Sing-Along CD: *You Can Be Anything:* Listen to the song and discuss the many things that the children in the class might like to play or try or be.

Understanding That People Can Change

2.7 PreK

OVERVIEW

Read and Discuss: *Growing, Learning, and Changing*

Explore and Practice: How We Change

GOALS

This set of activities is designed to:
- Foster incremental thinking—belief in the potential for flexibility and change in preferences, characteristics, abilities, and behaviors across time
- Promote motivation and persistence

LEARNING OBJECTIVES

Children will be able to:
- Describe ways that they have changed or will change.

KEY CONCEPTS AND VOCABULARY

People can change.

It is important to work hard and keep trying to learn new things.

Incremental (Change) Thinking Vocabulary to Use:
Grow
Learn
Change
Sometimes

Entity (Fixed) Thinking Vocabulary to Avoid:
Always
Never

MATERIALS

- *Growing, Learning, and Changing* storybook
- Paper and writing materials

Understanding That People Can Change

2.7 PreK

RESEARCH AND RELEVANCE

People who have an "entity theory" believe that personal characteristics (e.g., interests, abilities) are fixed and cannot be changed, and in turn expect that individuals will feel, think, and behave very consistently across time and situations. In addition, people with an entity view have stronger stereotypes than those with more flexible thinking, and often view members within a social group (such as gender or race) as extremely similar to one another and very different from members of other groups. In contrast, people who hold an "incremental theory" view personal characteristics as changeable through growth, effort, or learning. They believe that people are influenced by situational or psychological factors and tend to perceive more variability across members of a group than do entity thinkers. Thus, fostering incremental thinking in children can help them develop more flexible and less rigid social views and to be open to the possibility of change in themselves and others.

In addition, when these two types of thinking guide beliefs about ability, they can affect school achievement. For example, those who have an incremental view of intelligence and ability believe that these can be changed with effort, and may be more likely to see value in working toward improvement or trying other strategies. On the other hand, those with an entity theory tend to have diminished motivation in the face of challenge (because they believe there is nothing they can do to alter the outcome), and are at risk for helplessness and underachievement.

Think about this...

Has there ever been a time when your feelings or opinions about a matter of importance to you changed over time? Do you think that you would have been able to predict this change earlier?

What are your thoughts on the nature of such traits as emotionality, activity level, sociability, self-regulation, social competence, academic abilities, creative abilities—do you think they are generally "hard-wired" and fixed or that they are more learned/socialized and malleable? How do your views on these characteristics impact your beliefs, expectations, and interactions with the children in your classroom?

Try this today...

Promote incremental thinking, or belief in the potential for growth and change, by focusing on process rather than product—call attention to children's *efforts* rather than the *outcome* of those efforts, and help them reflect on and take ownership of their own learning and growth.

When children succeed:
Instead of saying: *You're really good at tying your shoes!*
Say: *You have been practicing tying your shoes over and over, and now you've finally done it by yourself!*

When children struggle:
Instead of saying: *It's okay, not everyone is good at drawing animals.*
Say: *Animals can be tough to draw. You're working so hard at it that I'm sure you're going to keep getting better and better at it!*

Understanding That People Can Change

2.7 PreK

READ AND DISCUSS: *GROWING, LEARNING, AND CHANGING*

Children discuss how everyone can change by learning new things, and the importance of persistence in working at learning something new.

Before Reading

What is something new that you have learned this year? Was it easy or hard for you to learn?

In this story, Z feels like Z will always have a hard time doing something and will never, ever be able to learn how to do it. The kids help Z learn that you are always growing and changing in many ways, and that by working and trying hard, you can learn a lot of new things.

As you listen to the story, pay attention to how Z feels about trying to learn something new that is hard.

During Reading

Why was Z excited to try and write Z's name? *(Z wanted to learn something new, wanted to write like Kenny, had never tried it before)*

Why do you think Z said that Z was no good at writing? *(It was hard, the crayons were breaking, Z couldn't write a Z very well)*

Do you think Z was really no good at writing? What did Z need to do instead? *(Keep trying, practice, calm down, try a different way)*

What happened after Z kept practicing? *(Z was able to write a Z, Z was happy to learn how to do it)*

What do you think might have happened if Z had stopped trying? *(Z would have felt sad, Z wouldn't have been able to write Z's name, Z might not have tried writing anything else)*

After Reading

Why is it important to keep trying, even when things are hard? *(You could learn how to do it, you can get better at it, you could figure out a new way to do it)*

What would happen if you gave up trying something new every time it seemed hard? *(You wouldn't learn new things; you might feel badly that you couldn't do some things)*

Understanding That People Can Change

2.7 PreK

EXPLORE AND PRACTICE: HOW WE CHANGE

Children discuss the ways and reasons that people can change in what they like, feel, and do, and describe and draw one way that they have changed.

Set the Stage

Discuss the concept of change.

Point out a variety of things in and around the classroom (*e.g., a chair, the classroom pet, a tree outside the window*) and discuss whether each of these things stays the same or can change, and why they can change (*e.g., grow bigger, leaves change with the seasons*).

Facilitate the Activity

Next, ask children if they think that people can change, and discuss some examples.

Think about what you were like when you were a baby. How are you different now? (*Learned how to talk and walk, are able to eat all kinds of foods, have younger brothers and sisters*).

Now think back to the beginning of the school year. How have you changed since then? (*Grew taller, made new friends, learned how to ride a bike*).

Summarize the idea of change in people.

Everyone changes in many ways, because everyone has the ability to grow and learn new things. You can also change because you decide that you want to be different. You might decide to change your mind about what you like or how you feel about something or what you like to do.

Have children sit with their buddies and briefly review some of the ways that they have changed since they were younger. Guide children in thinking about how they might change in the next year (e.g., *What is something new you might want to try? What is something you think you will learn? What do you think you will look like when you are five?*). Have children draw and dictate/write about one way that they think they will change. Encourage buddies to compare their work with one another, and then gather children back together to discuss with the class.

Tip: If children generate "creative" answers about change in inanimate objects, guide their understanding by asking if those objects could change "all by themselves".

Understanding That People Can Change

Wrap it Up

What would it be like if everyone was the same all the time and never changed?
(Boring, never get to be surprised, wouldn't be able to learn or try anything new, wouldn't be able to make new friends)

What would happen if you thought that you could never change or learn anything new?
(Wouldn't try anything new, wouldn't try to learn things)

SUPPLEMENTAL ACTIVITIES

Changing Role Play: Have children role play an activity (e.g., eating, swinging a baseball bat, marching) or emotion, then ask them to think of a different activity or emotion and change their action or expression to that. Invite the class to guess the new action.

Communication

Unit 3

Communication

3.0 — PreK

OVERVIEW

Unit 3 focuses on promoting comfort, self-confidence, and respect when children communicate with others and helping them develop and practice positive and successful communication skills.

GOALS

This unit is designed to help children:
- Develop skills for careful and thoughtful listening
- Develop respectful and reciprocal patterns of communication
- Gain positive and effective strategies for asserting their ideas, preferences, and needs

ACTIVITIES

3.1 Listening to Others
Children discuss the importance of being thoughtful and careful listeners, and practice how to use whole body listening skills (eyes looking, ears listening, mouth quiet, body still) during a song.

3.2 Responding to Others
Children discuss the importance of reciprocal communication and practice "talking back and forth" with a peer.

3.3 Being Assertive
Children discuss the importance of speaking up in a respectful way and practice Speaking Up, Speaking Kindly.

Home School Connection

Unit 3 — PreK

3.1 Listening to Others

Suggested information to share with families in the classroom newsletter:

Our class is talking about how to be a good listener to others (eyes looking, ears listening, mouth quiet, body still), and how this is respectful and shows that you care about what they are saying.

You may wish to:

- Ask your child how they use their whole body to be a careful listener.
- Brainstorm with your child to create a special signal that can remind or reinforce family members for good listening.
- Tell your child when you notice him/her demonstrating good listening skills.

3.2 Responding to Others

Suggested information to share with families in the classroom newsletter:

Our class is talking about how to be a good listener to others (eyes looking, ears listening, mouth quiet, body still), and how this is respectful and shows that you care about what they are saying.

You may wish to:

- Ask your child how they use their whole body to be a careful listener.
- Brainstorm with your child to create a special signal that can remind or reinforce family members for good listening.
- Tell your child when you notice him/her demonstrating good listening skills

3.3 Being Assertive

Suggested information to share with families in the classroom newsletter:

Our class is learning that it is important to speak up and share our ideas and feelings or ask for help, and we are practicing how to *Speak Up and Speak Kindly*.

You may wish to:

- Ask your child what kind of voice you use when you speak up.
- Ask your child what kind of words you use when you speak up.
- Tell your child when you notice him/her using a strong, respectful voice and kind words to speak up.

Listening to Others

3.1 PreK

OVERVIEW

Read and Discuss: *Being a Good Listener*

Explore and Practice: If You're Listening and You Know It

MATERIALS

- *Being a Good Listener* storybook
- *Whole Body Listening* cards

GOALS

This set of activities is designed to:
- Promote attentive listening skills.
- Foster self-regulation.

LEARNING OBJECTIVES

Children will be able to:
- Describe and demonstrate attentive listening.
- Identify examples of attentive listening.

KEY CONCEPTS AND VOCABULARY

Listening to others is important because:
- It shows that we care about what they are saying.
- It is respectful.
- We can learn about them.

To be a good listener:
- Look at the person who is speaking.
- Listen with your ears.
- Keep your voice quiet.
- Keep your body still.

If you don't hear or understand what others say, you can ask questions.

Listening to Others

3.1 — PreK

RESEARCH AND RELEVANCE

Being able to listen to others in a thoughtful and careful manner is critical for children's social and academic learning, allowing them to gain information and to develop vocabulary, comprehension, and oral language skills. Although young children make increasing strides in their abilities to self-regulate—including paying attention and controlling their bodies—there are a number of factors that can make it challenging for them to listen carefully. Environmental challenges can include external distractions such as noise and movement, which cannot always be controlled, and internal challenges may include comprehension difficulties, a lack of motivation or interest, or competing interests. It is important to provide children with many opportunities to practice focused, attentive listening and to help them monitor their own listening behavior and comprehension.

Think about this…

Have you ever found yourself not listening to a child or colleague? In what situations do you notice this happening?

How do you model respectful listening with the children in your classroom?

Try this today…

Be explicit in describing how you are modeling and engaging in attentive listening with children.

We can talk about your question as soon as I finish writing this note to myself, because I want to be able to give you my full attention.

Gina, would you please scoot a little to the left of where you're sitting? I want to make sure we can all see one another while we're talking.

Listening to Others

3.1 PreK

READ AND DISCUSS: BEING A GOOD LISTENER

Children listen to the story and discuss why it is important to listen to others and how to listen carefully using their whole body.

Before Reading

When are times when it is important for you to be a good listener? When can it be hard to be a good listener?

In this story, Z has a hard time listening. The kids help Z learn that it is important to be a good listener, and that you use your whole body to do that. You pay attention with your eyes and your ears, and you keep your voice quiet and your body still.

As you listen to the story, pay attention for times when Z forgets how to listen and for times when Z listens well.

During Reading

What should Z have done instead of interrupting Jeremy? *(Waited for Jeremy to finish talking, listened to Jeremy's story)*

If you wanted to say something while someone else was already talking, what could you do instead of interrupting them? *(Cross your fingers to remember what you want to say, find something to do while you wait, say "Excuse me" if it is something that cannot wait)*

How do you think Kim felt when Z wasn't listening to her? *(Sad, frustrated, ignored)*
How do you think she felt later when Z did listen to her? *(Happy, respected, like Z cared what she was saying)*

What are some ways Z learned that you can use your whole body to listen carefully to others? *(Look at the person, listen to what they are saying, keep voice quiet, keep body still)*

Tip: Remind children that some people use their eyes, ears, mouths, and bodies in different ways in order to listen and communicate (e.g., some people communicate with gestures).

After Reading

Why is it important to take turns talking and listening to others? *(It's fair, it gives everyone a chance to talk and listen, it gives everyone a chance to ask questions, you can hear everyone's ideas and stories)*

Listening to Others

3.1 PreK

What could happen if you weren't listening very well to what others were saying? *(They might think you don't care about what they are saying, you could miss out on something fun, you wouldn't hear directions, you won't learn things)*

What could you do if you forgot to listen or couldn't hear what someone was saying? *(Ask them to repeat what they said, ask questions)*

EXPLORE AND PRACTICE: IF YOU'RE LISTENING AND YOU KNOW IT

Children discuss how to pay attention and listen with your whole body using eyes, ears, mouth, and body, and then practice listening during a song.

Set the Stage

Explain that the class will be talking about good listening, and that you need a volunteer to help you show how to be a good listener. Invite a volunteer to stand next to you, and ask them a question that requires more than a brief answer (e.g., *What happened in the story we just read?*). As they reply, demonstrate poor listening in a silly, exaggerated manner (e.g., look around the room, hum loudly, turn and say hello to another child, walk around the volunteer, put your head down).

When finished, thank the class for listening to the volunteer, and ask them how you did at being a good listener, and how you could have listened better.

Facilitate the Activity

Discuss why it is important to listen to others and how to be a careful listener using your whole body.

Listening to others shows that we care about what they are saying and helps us learn and understand things. When we are paying attention and listening carefully to someone:
- Our eyes are looking at them,
- Our ears are listening to what they are saying,
- Our mouths are quiet,
- And our bodies are still.

Tip: Be sensitive to cultural differences in beliefs about appropriate eye contact when talking with someone.

Show the *Whole Body Listening* cards one at a time and have the class repeat them, and then demonstrate good listening with their whole body.

sanfordharmonyprogram.org ©Arizona State University All Rights Reserved

Listening to Others

3.1 PreK

Ask the class to listen carefully as you share 2-4 listening scenarios (refer to suggested scenarios below), and have children decide if the buddy is listening with their whole body or could listen better. If the buddy could listen better, invite a volunteer to select the *Whole Body Listening* card that the buddy needs to improve and to explain why.

Suggested Scenarios:

- *When you were talking to your buddy, she turned to look at you.*
- *When you asked your buddy for a crayon, she just kept looking down at her paper and coloring.*
- *While you were telling your buddy what you did last night, he stopped listening and thought about what he did last night.*
- *During circle time, your buddy sat still and listened to a classmate talk about his new puppy.*
- *When you were talking about a new movie you saw, your buddy interrupted to say that she wanted to see that movie too.*
- *Your buddy started coloring on her paper while the teacher was still explaining what to do.*

Next, have children stand and explain that you will be singing a song and that children will have to be good listeners in order to know what to do next in the song. Practice several verses of *If You're Listening and You Know It* with the class, singing and performing the movements instructed in the song.

If You're Listening and You Know It
If you're listening and you know it, clap your hands
If you're listening and you know it, clap your hands
If you're listening and you know it
Then you'll really want to show it
If you're listening and you know it, clap your hands

Variations:
Stomp your feet
Wiggle your fingers
Snap your fingers
Stretch up high
Touch your toes
Make a smile

Wrap it Up

What are the four ways that we use our whole body to be a careful listener? *(Listen with our ears, look with our eyes, keep our mouth quiet, and body still)*

How does it help our class when everyone is being a good listener? *(We can hear each other, we know what to do next, we show that we care about what the speaker is saying, we can learn things)* When can we practice being good listeners to each other this week?

Extension: Have children draw and write/dictate how they will be good listeners at school.

Listening to Others

3.1

SUPPLEMENTAL ACTIVITIES

If You're Listening (With Your Whole Body) and You Know It: Sing and act out the song, but add challenges by including both verbal and nonverbal instructions (model first with a volunteer). For each verse, alternate between verbally naming or silently demonstrating the movements so that children have to use their eyes and ears to follow the instructions.

Listen and Guess: Have children close their eyes. Make various sounds (e.g., shake a water bottle, drum your fingernails, turn the pages of a book), one at a time, and have children guess the sound.

Listen and Match: As you name each of the four body parts associated with good listening, ask children to name and demonstrate the corresponding listening skill. Then try naming each body part using a different loudness or tone of voice, and have children respond by naming the skill using a matching tone.

Listening Challenge: Before reading a story, give children 1-3 pieces of information to pay attention for during the story (it may help to have a related prop or a visual of the needed information). After the story, discuss what children heard.

The Waiting Game: Discuss times when children have to wait before they can speak to someone (e.g., *when the other person is already talking, when it is not your turn to speak, when the person is talking or listening to someone else, when the person is busy and can't listen to you*), and talk about how sometimes it might be hard to listen and think about what someone is saying because you are thinking about what *you* want to say. Brainstorm strategies for waiting to talk. Ask children a question (e.g., *Where would you like to visit on vacation?*) and encourage them to listen carefully to your own answer while they wait to share their answers. Have children listen for 5 or 10 seconds as you describe your answer, then have them turn to their buddy and share their answers. Try a few more times, lengthening the waiting period.

Z Sing-Along CD: *Good Listener:* Listen (like a good listener!) to the song and discuss how to be a good listener to everyone you meet.

Body Still

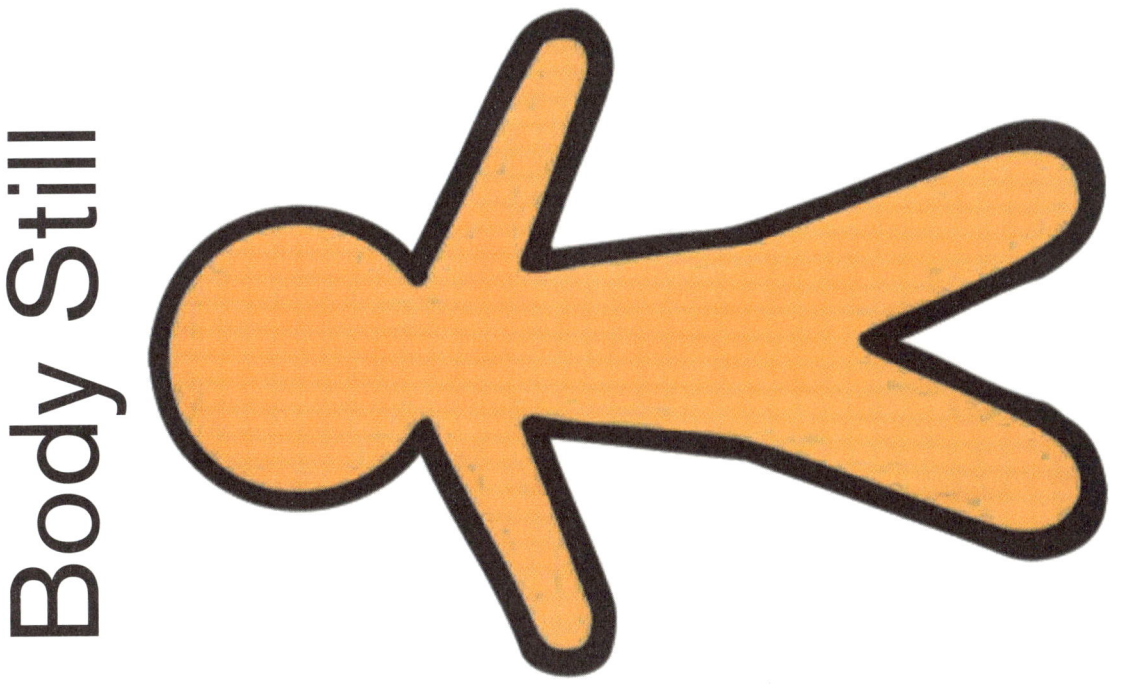

3.1 Whole Body Listening Cards
(PreK)

Ears Listening

Eyes Looking

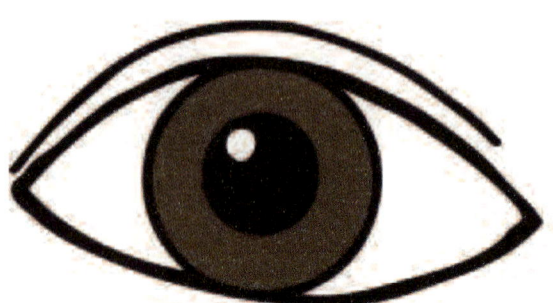 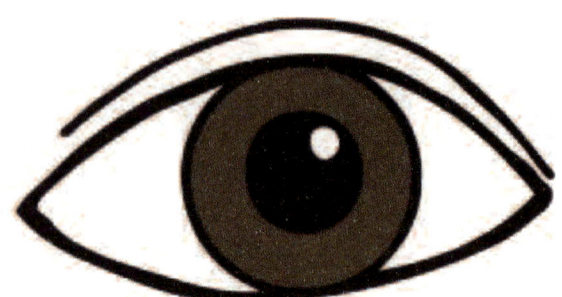

Mouth Quiet

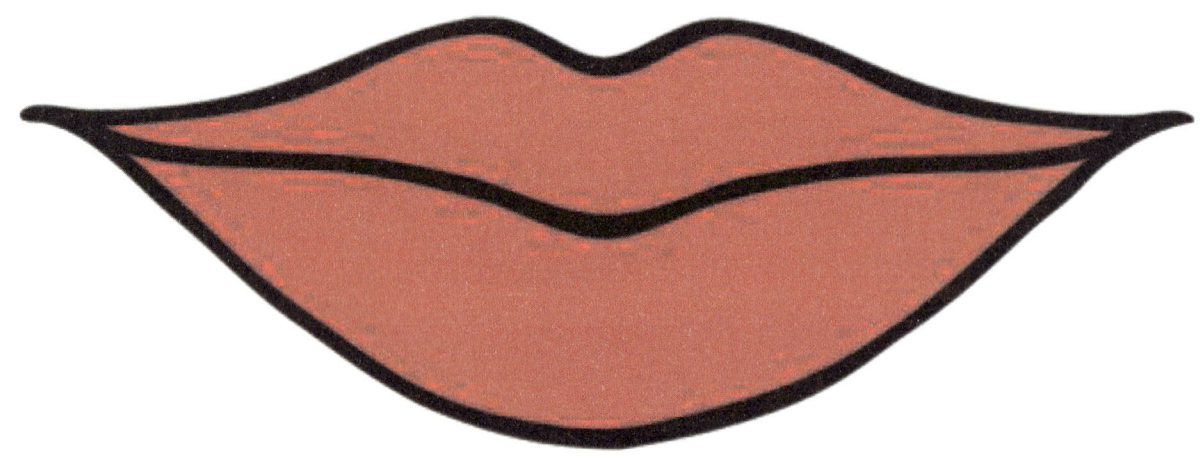

3.1 Whole Body Listening Cards
(PreK)

Talking Together

3.2 PreK

OVERVIEW

Read and Discuss: *Talking Back and Forth*

Explore and Practice: Back and Forth Buddies

GOALS

This set of activities is designed to:
- Promote reciprocal communication skills.
- Foster self-regulation.

LEARNING OBJECTIVES

Children will be able to:
- Demonstrate taking turns listening and talking with a partner.

KEY CONCEPTS AND VOCABULARY

It is important to *listen* carefully, *think* about what the person is saying, and *respond* to them.

To *respond* means to answer someone by saying or doing something after they speak to you.

Responding to others is important because it lets the person know:
- That you listened to them.
- That you thought about what they said.

It is fair to take turns speaking and listening.

MATERIALS

- *Talking Back and Forth* storybook
- Balls or small objects to pass (e.g., beanbags, talking sticks; one per buddy pair)

Talking Together   3.2

RESEARCH AND RELEVANCE

Responding to others can be an often-overlooked communication skill. In addition to listening attentively, it is important for children to understand that it is considerate to acknowledge that someone has spoken to you by responding verbally or behaviorally. Being able to engage in reciprocal, "back and forth" communication is critical for being able to maintain conversations with others.

Think about this…

Have you ever found yourself having a hard time really listening to someone, because you were thinking about the next thing you wanted to say? What strategies do you use to help yourself focus on your partner's words when you are eager for your turn to speak?

Have you ever found yourself listening carefully to a child or colleague, but not explicitly acknowledging (verbally or non-verbally) that you have heard them? In what situations do you notice this happening?

How do you model appropriate responding with the children in your classroom?

Try this today…

Be explicit in reinforcing children when they use reciprocal communication skills such as responding to one another and talking in turns.

I noticed that when Ginger said 'hello' to you, you turned to her and said 'hi' right back. I'll bet that made her feel good that you answered her.

I hear everyone at the blue table sharing some really great stories about your favorite place to go on vacation. Because you're all listening so carefully, everyone is getting a turn to tell their story.

Talking Together

3.2 PreK

READ AND DISCUSS: TALKING BACK AND FORTH

Children listen to the story and discuss why it is important to respond to others and to take turns speaking and listening.

Before Reading

If you were talking with a friend, what could happen if you both wanted to talk at the same time, all the time?

In this story, Z doesn't understand how to go back and forth when you talk to someone. The kids help Z learn how to listen and then respond, and how to take turns talking.

As you listen to the story, pay attention to what happens when Z is talking with the kids and forgets to take turns.

During Reading

To *respond* means to answer someone by saying or doing something after they speak to you. **How do you think the kids felt when they talked to Z, and Z didn't respond?** *(Sad, ignored, didn't know if Z heard them)* **Why is it important to respond when someone speaks to you?** *(So they know you listened to them, so they know you care about what they said)*

Was it fair for Z to keep talking and talking about animals instead of giving the kids a turn to speak? **If Z just didn't give the kids a turn to talk, how do you think they might feel?** *(Sad, bored, wouldn't want to talk to Z anymore)*

After Reading

Why is it important to take turns talking and listening to others? *(It's fair, it gives everyone a chance to talk and listen, it gives everyone a chance to ask questions, you can hear everyone's ideas and stories)*

When someone talks to you, what are some ways you can respond to let them know that you heard and thought about what they said? *(Answer with words, nod, shake our head, smile or wave back at them, do what the person asked)*

Tip: Provide a prompt if necessary (e.g., *How could you respond if someone said hello to you?*)

Talking Together

3.2

EXPLORE AND PRACTICE: BACK AND FORTH BUDDIES

Children practice taking turns listening and speaking as they talk with a buddy.

Set the Stage

Gather children into a circle with their buddies. Explain that you and the class are going to take turns and go back and forth saying a rhyme together, and that you will begin and that they should listen carefully and think about what you are saying. When you point to them, they should respond with what comes next. Recite a familiar rhyme or chant, stopping and pointing to children so they can respond by filling in key words.

Twinkle, twinkle, little [point]
How I wonder what you [point].
Up above the world so [point],
Like a diamond in the [point].

Ask children if it would have been hard to respond if they weren't listening and thinking about what you were saying.

Facilitate the Activity

Review the importance of taking turns speaking and listening, thinking, and responding.

When you are talking with someone, it is important to go back and forth and to take turns speaking and listening. That is fair because everyone has a chance to say things and to listen to what others have to say. When it is your turn to listen, you should listen carefully, think about what the person is saying, and then respond back to them.

Explain that children will be talking back and forth with their buddies. With a volunteer, model passing a ball back and forth as you take turns talking about a topic (e.g., *what you had for breakfast*), and ask children to pay attention and let you know if you forget to take turns. "Forget" a couple of times by continuing to hold the ball and 1) talking for a long time, or 2) not responding at all. Point out how the volunteer is being a good listener when you are speaking.

Have children sit and face their buddies and give each pair a ball. Have children demonstrate how they will look when they are being good listeners to one another. Explain that the child holding the ball should speak and then roll the ball to their buddy. When their buddy receives the ball, it is their turn to speak and then roll it back.

Talking Together

3.2 PreK

Provide a topic (e.g., favorite movie), monitor buddy exchanges, and end the conversation after a short time. Repeat with another topic as time allows.

Have buddies face the group again and invite children to share with the class some things they learned about their buddy.

Tip: Let children know when they can each have one more turn and pass of the ball before time ends.

Wrap it Up

How did you make sure that you and your buddy both had a chance to talk and to listen? *(Took turns, listened to each other)*

Was it hard for you to wait for your turn to talk? What did you do while you waited? *(Listened, thought about what their buddy was saying, looked at their buddy)*

SUPPLEMENTAL ACTIVITIES

Back and Forth Chants: Split the class into two groups facing one another and lead children in a familiar chant, having half the class begin the chant and then the other half 1) repeat the words, or 2) say the next part of the chant.

Z Sing-Along CD: *Good Listener*: Listen to the song and discuss how to take turns and "talk about you, talk about me".

Being Assertive

3.3 PreK

OVERVIEW

Read and Discuss: *Our Words Are Important*

Explore and Practice: Speak Up, Speak Kindly

MATERIALS

- *Our Words Are Important* storybook

GOALS

This set of activities is designed to:
- Foster self-confidence in communicating needs, desires, and ideas.
- Promote assertiveness skills.

LEARNING OBJECTIVES

Children will be able to:
- Identify situations in which it is appropriate or inappropriate to speak up.
- Demonstrate respectful, assertive speaking.

KEY CONCEPTS AND VOCABULARY

You can speak up with others because your ideas and feelings are important to share.

When you *speak up and speak kindly* you:
- Stand tall.
- Look at the person.
- Use a strong, respectful voice.
- Use kind words.

If someone doesn't hear or understand you, you can try again or try a different way.

Being Assertive

3.3

RESEARCH AND RELEVANCE

For social interactions to be successful, children must not only practice good listening, but also be able to communicate to others effectively. Sometimes it can be challenging or uncomfortable for children to speak up appropriately and this can prevent them from having their ideas, desires, and needs from being heard, acknowledged, and addressed. Some children may be more quiet, timid, or passive, and may need support in developing the self-confidence to express themselves assertively. Other children may be more loud, boisterous, or aggressive, and may need support in speaking respectfully so that others will listen. In other cases, there can be a mismatch in communication styles between children. Some children may be more direct in their expressions (e.g., *I need that red crayon that you have.* or *Please hand me that red crayon.*), whereas other children may have a more indirect manner (e.g., *Can I please use that red crayon?* or *I don't have a red crayon to use.*). Children might find that their communication attempts are successful with some peers but less effective with other peers who have different expressive styles.

Children need to feel that their words and ideas are important. Self-confidence in speaking up is enhanced when children feel that they are in a safe, respectful environment and when they see that others around them acknowledge and value what they say and respond to them. Being able to communicate effectively also fosters a sense of self-agency—the feeling that they can and do have some influence and control within their social environment and interactions—and that will motivate them to engage in these interactions with others again.

Think about this…
Do you find any particular communication behaviors more challenging for yourself—listening thoughtfully, waiting to share your own ideas, speaking up with your ideas? What contexts make these behaviors more difficult?

Try this today…
Reinforce children for speaking assertively, and provide scaffolding for those who may be more passive or reluctant to speak up in a group.

> *You all have some great ideas about what might happen next in the story. Let's make sure to hear from everyone—what do you think will happen, Lisa?*

> *You look like you might have an idea, Christina. Would you like to share what you're thinking?*

> *I heard Christian remind everyone to wait quietly in line, and then I noticed that you all stopped chatting. It was good that he spoke up in such a clear, strong voice so that everyone could hear and be reminded.*

Being Assertive

3.3 PreK

READ AND DISCUSS: *OUR WORDS ARE IMPORTANT*

Children listen to the story and discuss why it is important to speak up, and when and how speaking up is appropriate.

Before Reading

Have you had a great idea that you wanted to tell someone? What did you do?

In this story, Z doesn't want to tell the kids an idea because Z is feeling shy and it doesn't seem like anyone is listening. The kids help Z learn that it's okay to speak up, because everyone has important things to say.

As you listen to the story, pay attention to what Z does when Z has an idea, and if these things worked or didn't work.

During Reading

What happened when Z just pointed at the green button? *(The kids didn't know what Z was trying to say)* What happened when Z just whispered about the green button? *(The kids didn't hear)*

Is it okay to speak up with an idea, even if it might not work or be the best idea? Why? *(Everyone's ideas are important, everyone should get a chance to share their ideas and feelings)*

What did Z finally do so that the kids heard the idea about the green button? *(Spoke up, used a strong voice)*

What if Z hadn't ever spoken up about the green button—what could have happened? *(They wouldn't have known how to fix the bubble machine, Z would have felt badly, they wouldn't have gotten to play with the bubbles)*

After Reading

When are some times that you might need to speak up to someone? *(When you need help, when you want something, when you have an idea, when you want to play with someone)*

What could you do if you tried to speak up and no one heard you? *(Say it again, say it in a louder, respectful voice, say the person's name, wave or tap someone softly to get their attention, ask an adult for help speaking up)*

Being Assertive

3.3 PreK

Do you think it is okay to speak up and say anything at all that you want to say? What kind of words should you use when you speak up? *(Kind words, respectful words)*

Tip: Emphasize to children that they can *Speak Up, Speak Kindly.*

EXPLORE AND PRACTICE: SPEAK UP, SPEAK KINDLY

Children discuss when it is appropriate to speak up to others, and practice how to Speak Up, Speak Kindly.

Set the Stage

Tell children that you have something fun that you would like to talk about with them (e.g., a book or activity to be introduced later in the day). Pause silently and wait for children to question you, prompting them if they don't respond (*Do you think I should tell you?*). Next, whisper or mumble what you have to say, or speak with your head down. Wait, and prompt if necessary (*Could you hear what I said to you?*). Discuss why it is important to speak up when you have something to share (*you can tell your ideas, others will know what you want to say*).

Facilitate the Activity

Discuss why it is important to *speak up and speak kindly*.

Everyone has things to say, and it is important to know that you can speak up and tell others what you think, feel, or need. When you speak up, it is important to speak kindly. That way you can share your thoughts and feelings with others, but you also respect their thoughts and feelings.

Have children face their buddies and practice each skill as you describe and model each aspect of *speaking up and speaking kindly*.

- √ **Stand tall.**
    - ▶ Standing tall helps you speak clearly.
    - ▶ Have children stand (or sit) with their head up and shoulders back.
- √ **Look at the person.**
    - ▶ It is important to look at your buddy so they know you are speaking to them.
    - ▶ Have buddies stand tall and look at one another.

Tip: Be aware of cultural differences in beliefs about appropriate eye contact when talking with someone.

Being Assertive

3.3 PreK

√ **Use a strong, friendly voice.**
- ▸ It is important to use a clear, strong, and friendly tone of voice.
- ▸ Demonstrate speaking in different tones, and ask children to decide if your voice is not strong enough or too strong.
- ▸ Have buddies stand tall, look at one another, and practice speaking with a strong, clear voice (e.g., *Hi, buddy!*).

√ **Use kind words.**
- ▸ It is okay to say when you have an idea or you want something or you need help, but that it is not okay to say things that are hurtful to others.
- ▸ Have buddies stand tall, look at one another, use a strong voice, and say something kind to one another (e.g., *I think you're great because_____.*). Remind partners to respond (e.g., *Thank you.*).

Tip: Establish a system for which buddy will speak first.

Have children face the group again in a circle.

Now you are going to have a chance to speak up and speak kindly to the whole class, just like you did with your buddy. When your classmates are speaking, listen carefully and think about what the person is saying.

Share a "speaking up" scenario (refer to suggested scenarios below) and ask the class if it is okay to speak up in that situation. If so, go around the circle and have several children demonstrate what they would say in a clear, strong, kind, voice (if not okay, discuss why). Choose additional scenarios and continue around the circle so that each child has an opportunity to practice speaking up.

Speaking Up Scenarios
You want to play with a classmate.
You don't like your friend's drawing. (not okay)
You like your friend's drawing.
You need help opening the glue.
You didn't hear what you are supposed to do next.
You think it is silly that your classmate is afraid of dogs. (not okay)
You see a classmate get hurt on the playground.
You would like a turn on the swings.

Wrap it Up

How did you make sure that you and your buddy both had a chance to talk and to listen? *(Took turns, listened to each other)*

Was it hard for you to wait for your turn to talk? What did you do while you waited?
(Listened, thought about what their buddy was saying, looked at their buddy)

Being Assertive

SUPPLEMENTAL ACTIVITIES

Say It Loud, Say It Proud: Gather children into a circle and pass around a "microphone", giving each child an opportunity to briefly share about a topic (e.g., something they would like to do this weekend) and practice assertive speaking.

Problem Solving

Unit 4

Problem Solving

4.0 PreK

OVERVIEW

Unit 4 focuses on fostering children's ability to resolve conflicts and to work cooperatively and compatibly with others.

GOALS

This unit is designed to help children:
- Accept and value different feelings and perspectives.
- Develop empathy.
- Identify and generate solutions to interpersonal problems.
- Develop cooperation skills.
- Understand how to compromise with others.
- Practice self-regulation.

ACTIVITIES

4.1 Identifying Problems
Children discuss the first two steps in solving problems (Stop, Talk), and practice identifying and stating problems presented in scenarios.

4.2 Solving Problems
Children discuss the last two steps in solving problems (Think, Try), practice generating solutions to problems presented in scenarios, and then problem-solve with a peer during collaborative play.

4.3 Cooperating
Children discuss teamwork skills and work together on a collaborative construction activity.

4.4 Being Considerate
Children discuss being considerate of others and practice strategies for self-regulation during a song.

Home-School Connections — Unit 4 PreK

4.1 Identifying Problems

Suggested information to share with families in the classroom newsletter:

Our class is talking about how it's okay for people to have different feelings or ideas about the same thing or the same situation, and how we can disagree with one another respectfully. We are learning that it is important to talk to each other so that we know how everyone feels and thinks and can understand the problem.

When you have a problem or disagreement, you can:
- ▶ *STOP and calm down*
- ▶ *TALK about each person's perspective so you understand the problem*
- ▶ *THINK of possible solutions*
- ▶ *TRY a solution and see how it works for everyone*

You may wish to:

- Talk with your child about the first two steps to solving a problem (**Stop, Talk**).
- Encourage your child to use calming strategies (e.g., taking deep breaths, counting slowly, thinking of something beautiful, hugging a stuffed animal) when they are upset or overexcited.
- Take opportunities, while reading stories or watching videos that involve a conflict or difference of opinion, to guide your child in recognizing each person's perspective and in using words to label the problem (e.g., *She wants to pull her friend in the wagon but he is excited to ride bikes, so it seems like the problem they're having is that they don't want to do the same thing*.). This gives children practice in developing empathy and in identifying problems in situations in which they are not involved (and possibly already feeling upset).

4.2 Solving Problems

Suggested information to share with families in the classroom newsletter:

Our class is talking about how it's okay for people to have different ideas about how to solve a problem. We are learning that it is fair to listen to everyone's ideas and work together to choose a solution that makes everyone feel okay.

When you have a problem or disagreement, you can:
- ▶ *STOP and calm down*
- ▶ *TALK about each person's perspective so you understand the problem*
- ▶ *THINK of possible solutions*
- ▶ *TRY a solution and see how it works for everyone*

Home-School Connections — Unit 4 PreK

4.3 Cooperating

Suggested information to share with families in the classroom newsletter:

Our class is talking about what it means to be fair and cooperate when you are playing or working with others, and we are doing some activities that give everyone a chance to work as a team.

You may wish to:

- Ask your child about some of the things that are important to do when you work together (e.g., include everyone, listen and cooperate, use kind words).
- Talk with your child about the ways that your family cooperates with one another (e.g., making dinner, washing the car, putting together a puzzle, etc.), and discuss how much fun it can be to work together and how everyone helps to get the job completed.
- Tell your child when you notice him/her using teamwork skills and point out how it is helpful (e.g., *I saw how carefully you were listening to Grandma explain how to pat the soil down around the plant, and the garden looks great after all your hard work today!*).

4.4 Being Considerate

Suggested information to share with families in the classroom newsletter:

Our class is talking about how sometimes we can be very excited and active, and other times we can be very calm and still. We are learning ways to change our behavior when it is necessary so that we can respect and get along with others around us.

You may wish to:

- Ask your child what it means to "have the ziggles" and how to turn them up or down.
- Play games that help your child practice self-regulation, or changing their behavior on purpose:
  - Alternate between counting to 10 very quickly, and then very slowly.
  - Play music and dance excitedly, and then begin to dance more slowly as you turn down the volume.
- Brainstorm with your child to create a special signal (e.g., palms facing up/down to indicate "turn it up" or "turn it down") that can provide them with a gentle reminder to adjust their behavior (e.g., "pump it up" or calm down), and help them practice doing this.
- Tell your child when you notice him/her intentionally calming down, and talk about how that feels.

Identifying Problems

4.1 PreK

OVERVIEW

Read and Discuss: *Different Feelings Are Okay*

Explore and Practice: Spot the Problem

GOALS

This set of activities is designed to:
- Promote skills in recognizing and identifying interpersonal problems.
- Encourage self-confidence in sharing feelings and ideas.
- Foster awareness and acceptance of different feelings and perspectives.

LEARNING OBJECTIVES

Children will be able to:
- Name the first two steps in problem-solving (Stop, Talk).
- Identify multiple perspectives and state the problem in a given scenario.

KEY CONCEPTS AND VOCABULARY

It's okay to disagree if you feel differently than someone else.

When you have a problem or disagreement, you can:
- **STOP** and calm down.
- **TALK** so you can understand and say the problem.
- **THINK** of possible solutions.
- **TRY** a solution and see how it works for everyone.

MATERIALS
- *Different Feelings Are Okay* storybook
- *Problem-Solving* poster
- *Spot the Problem* scenarios

Identifying Problems   4.1

RESEARCH AND RELEVANCE

Conflicts are a natural part of social interactions—people often have different feelings, perspectives, or ideas. Young children often need additional support in negotiating conflicts with peers, because they often have difficulty taking another's perspective (particularly when upset), and this can make it hard for them to think of solutions that will be mutually satisfying for everyone involved. One strategy that children might use is to avoid conflict by going along with what others want, even if it does not make them feel okay. Avoiding conflict does not solve the problem—children should feel comfortable expressing their ideas and feelings respectfully, even when they are different from those of others.

Adults can provide support by guiding children to stop and regain calmness, to talk about each person's feelings and perspectives so that they can identify the problem, to generate possible solutions and potential consequences, and to choose and try a course of action and see how it works. Younger children will usually only be able to do these steps in simple forms and with adult facilitation. With time and practice, these steps can become more detailed and nuanced, as children's social interactions become more complex as well. Eventually, children will develop the flexible capability to begin to resolve peer disputes without assistance.

What You Can Do To Problem Solve

Children can:	Adults can:
STOP *and calm down*	Remain calm, acknowledge and label how children feel, help them use calming strategies
TALK *about the situation and state the problem*	*Gather information by asking children's perspectives on the situation, guide children in stating the problem*

Think about this…

Have you ever ended up in a conflict because of missing or misunderstanding someone else's feelings or perspective? Did you ever not even realize that there was a problem?

When a friend or colleague does not share the same opinion on a matter of importance to you, how likely are you to feel that this person is "wrong"? How hard do you try to accept or understand their opinion, and/or to explain or convince them of the "right" perspective?

What strategies do you find effective in working with people whose ideas or feelings differ from your own?

Try this today…

When reading stories or discussing events that have happened (e.g., a story that a child is sharing with the class) that involve a conflict or difference of opinion, take opportunities to guide children in recognizing each person's perspective and in using words to label the problem. This helps children develop empathy and gives them practice in identifying problems in situations in which they are not currently involved and feeling upset.

What did the older child want to do with her drawing? How did she feel when her little brother scribbled on it? Do you think he meant to ruin her picture and make her angry? Why do you think he scribbled on it? So it sounds like the problem is that her brother likes to scribble on paper, but sometimes he scribbles on her drawings when they are left on the table.

Identifying Problems

4.1

READ AND DISCUSS: DIFFERENT FEELINGS ARE OKAY

Children listen to the story and discuss how to STOP and calm down, and then TALK to one another so that you can understand a problem and work together to find a solution.

Before Reading

Think about a time when you were playing with a friend and you each wanted to do something different. What happened?

In this story, Z doesn't want to do what the kids want to do, so they help Z learn that it's okay to disagree and have different feelings and ideas. When you have a disagreement, you can stop and talk about the problem so you can figure out how to solve it together.

As you listen to the story, pay attention to how Z and the kids feel differently so you can spot their problem.

During Reading

How did the kids feel about going outside to splash in the puddles? *(Excited, happy)* How did Z feel about doing this? *(Worried, sad)* Do you think this will be a problem for playing together?

Why did Z agree to go outside with the kids? *(Z knew they were excited to go outside, didn't want them to be upset)* If Z would have gone outside at first, without saying the problem, what could have happened? *(Z could have gotten wet and cold, wouldn't have had fun, could have felt sad or angry)*

When Z and the kids finally figured out that they disagreed, what is the first thing that they did? *(<u>Stopped</u>)* Why is important to stop first when there is a disagreement? *(So you can calm down, so you can think clearer)* **What are some ways that you can calm yourself down?** *(Take a deep breath, count to five, think of something that makes you happy)*

After they stopped, what is the next thing that they did? *(<u>Talked</u> and listened to each other so they could figure out the problem)*

What was the problem that Z and the kids had? *(They wanted to do different things; they didn't feel the same way about playing in puddles)*

What was their solution? *(The kids gave Z a raincoat and boots to wear outside so Z could stay dry and warm)* Was this a good solution? Why? *(They all agreed on the solution, everyone felt okay about it, the kids got to go outside and Z didn't get wet)*

Extension: Have children practice taking a deep breath and letting their body relax

Identifying Problems

4.1 PreK

After Reading

Why is it important to share your feelings and ideas, even if you disagree with someone else? *(Everyone's feelings and ideas are important, it helps people understand one another, you can figure out how to solve the problem)*

Why is it important to stop and calm down before you talk about a problem? *(So you can listen to each other, so you can speak kindly to each other)*

Extension: Have children turn to their buddies and practice disagreeing by *Speaking Up* and *Speaking Kindly* in a strong, respectful voice (e.g., *I disagree, I have a different idea, I feel differently*).

EXPLORE AND PRACTICE: SPOT THE PROBLEM

Children discuss the first two steps in solving problems (Stop, Talk), and practice identifying and stating problems presented in scenarios.

Set the Stage

Share a real class scenario and ask if children think this would be a problem (e.g., *We only have one cape in the theater box. What if two kids both want to wear the cape at the same time? Would this be a problem?*).

Discuss the first two steps in solving a problem, referring to the *Problem-Solving* poster.

[STOP] Sometimes when you are having a disagreement or problem with someone, you might be feeling upset or angry. The first thing to do is to <u>stop</u> and calm down. When you are feeling calm again, you will be able to talk and listen to each other. So what is the first thing to do when you have a problem? *(Stop and calm down)*

[TALK] After you are calm, the second thing to do is to <u>talk</u> to each other about what is happening so you can understand the problem. You can say how you feel and listen to how the other person feels. When you figure out the problem, you can say what it is out loud. So what do you do together to figure out the problem? *(Talk to each other)*

Tip: Remind children of classroom guidelines for expressing angry feelings (e.g., It is okay to be angry and talk about it, but it isn't okay to hurt people or property).

Facilitate the Activity

Explain that the class will talk about some different situations that might happen between children and try to "spot the problem".

Identifying Problems

4.1 PreK

Guide children in discussing the *Spot the Problem* scenarios. Have children share answers with their buddies before inviting a few to share with the class. Read each scenario and:

- Identify the characters' feelings and what they could do to calm down.
- Identify each character's goals or thoughts.
- State the problem in words.
- Briefly discuss 1-2 possible solutions.

Wrap It Up

What is the first thing to do when you are having a problem with someone else? *(Stop and calm down)*

After you stop and calm down, what do you do next when you have a problem? *(Talk and listen to each other about how you each feel)*

Why is it important for everyone to be able to tell their feelings about the situation? *(Everyone's feelings and ideas are important; it helps you figure out the problem and think of different solutions)*

....

SUPPLEMENTAL ACTIVITIES

Agree/Disagree Game: Play a game in which you make a statement (e.g., *I love chocolate ice cream.*) and have children indicate whether they agree or disagree by giving a thumbs up, thumbs down, or flat hand (for "not sure"). Each time, ask for a volunteer from each group (agree, disagree, or not sure) to talk about their opinion, reminding them to use respectful and positive statements (e.g., say *I like strawberry ice cream best!* rather than saying *Chocolate ice cream is disgusting!*). Emphasize that everyone has different opinions sometimes and it is important to express your opinions and differences respectfully.

Disagree Respectfully Role Play: Discuss some conflict scenarios and invite children to role play the scenario and demonstrate respectful and assertive ways to disagree, using a strong voice, kind words, and respecting the other person's feelings or ideas.

- *You and a friend are building with blocks together. Your friend wants to add more blocks and build their tower really high, but you think that it might fall.*
- *A friend shows you a new game she got for her birthday and says, "This game is the best game ever!" You don't like that game at all.*
- *You and a friend are making pretend food out of clay together. Your friend wants to start making animals out of the clay instead, but you want to keep making food.*

Identifying Problems

4.1

What's the Problem Scenarios: Use puppets or stuffed animals to act out brief problem-solving situations. Guide children in identifying how each of the characters feel and how to calm down, and what each of them want. Have children state the problem in words, and then brainstorm possible solutions.

- *Two children reach for the same truck at the same time.*
- *One child wants to put stickers on their shared paper, but their buddy wants to use markers.*
- *One child accidentally knocks down another child's block tower.*

STOP

sanford harmony program

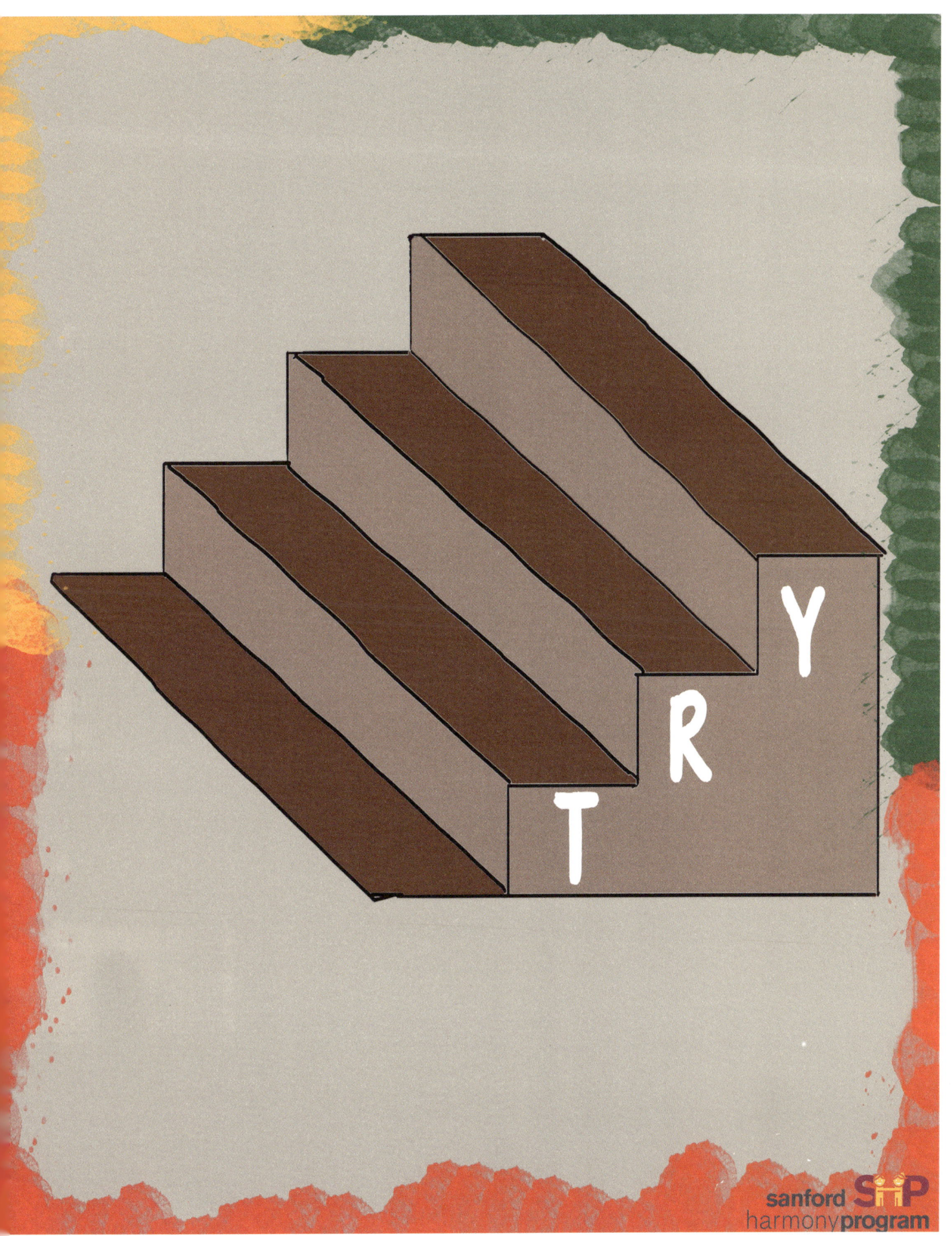

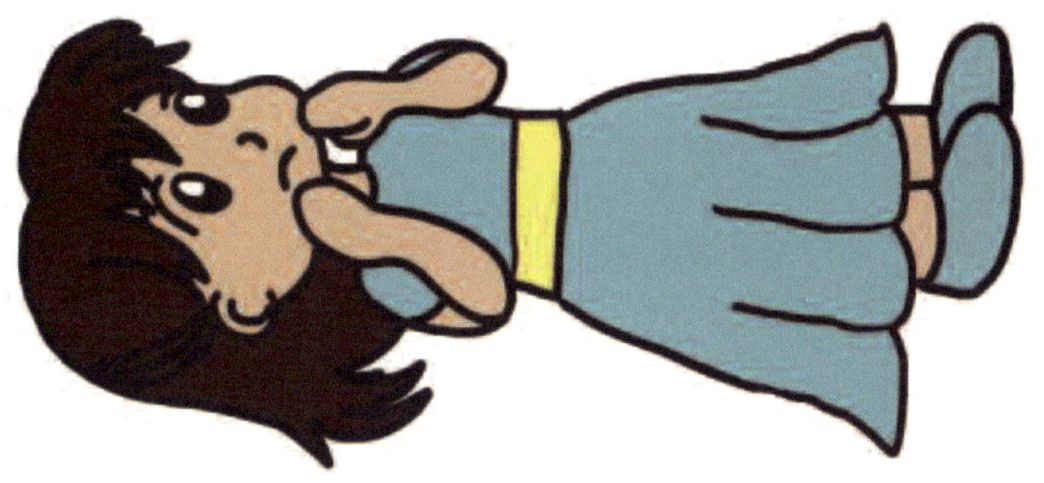

Mia is building a big tower with blocks and Kenny is playing Follow the Leader in the same area. Kenny doesn't see Mia's tower as he marches by and knocks it all down.

STOP

How do you think Mia might feel? *(Angry, sad, disappointed)*

What should Mia do first so they can solve the problem? *(Stop and calm down)*

What could she do to calm down? *(Take a deep breath, take a break)*

TALK

Once Mia stops and calms down, she and Kenny can talk about the problem.

What do you think Mia wants? *(To build a block tower)*

What do you think Kenny wants? *(To play Follow the Leader)*

What is the problem that Mia and Kenny have? *(They want to play different things in the same area)*

THINK, TRY

Mia and Kenny are trying to play different things in the same area, and now Mia's tower is ruined. What are some things that they could do to solve this problem? *(Kenny could help fix her tower; one person could play in a new area)*

Kim and Jordan are drawing. Kim is going to draw with the purple crayon, but Jordan reaches for it at the same time and says that he is going to use it now

STOP

How do you think Kim might feel? *(Upset, disappointed, confused)*

What should Kim do first so they can solve the problem? *(Stop and calm down)*

What could she do to calm down? *(Take a deep breath, count to five)*

TALK

Once Kim stops and calms down, she and Jordan can talk about the problem.

What do you think Kim wants? *(To use the purple crayon)*

What do you think Jordan wants? *(To use the purple crayon)*

What is the problem that Kim and Jordan have? *(They both want to use the same crayon)*

THINK, TRY

Kim and Jordan both want to use the same crayon. What are some things that they could do to solve this problem? *(Take turns with it, find another crayon, choose another color to use)*

©Arizona State University All Rights Reserved

4.1 Spot the Problem scenarios p. 2 (PreK)

Solving Problems

4.2 PreK

OVERVIEW

Read and Discuss: *Deciding Together*

Explore and Practice: Buddy Buckets

GOALS

This set of activities is designed to:
- Promote skills in generating solutions to interpersonal problems.
- Foster awareness that people can have different ideas about how to solve a problem.
- Emphasize fairness in problem-solving and decision-making.

LEARNING OBJECTIVES

Children will be able to:
- Name the last two steps in problem-solving (Think, Try).
- Generate fair solutions to given scenarios.
- Practice solving problems during play with a peer.

KEY CONCEPTS AND VOCABULARY

There can be more than one way to solve a problem.

Everyone's ideas and feelings are important, so it is fair to decide together.

A good solution makes everyone feel okay.

When you have a problem or disagreement, you can:
- **STOP** and calm down.
- **TALK** so you can understand and say the problem.
- **THINK** of possible solutions.
- **TRY** a solution and see how it works for everyone.

MATERIALS

- *Deciding Together* storybook
- *Problem-Solving* poster
- Containers with collections of various small toys (a "Buddy Bucket" for each buddy pair)

Solving Problems

4.2 PreK

RESEARCH AND RELEVANCE

Young children can often have a hard time thinking about the feelings and perspectives of others because they tend to focus on one thing at a time, and on the more concrete (rather than internal) aspects of a conflict situation. Sometimes a focus on their own needs and feelings can lead children to behave in ways that seem controlling or bossy, and this can make it difficult to resolve conflicts among peers. When conflicts occur in the classroom, they provide learning opportunities in which adults can guide children through the process of peaceful and effective problem-solving. Helping children develop positive strategies for resolving their day-to-day conflicts with peers will help prevent them from developing unhealthy patterns of behavior that could lead to social difficulties later in life. Other children benefit as well as they observe examples of positive conflict resolution.

What You Can Do To Problem Solve

Children can:	Adults can:
THINK of possible solutions	Encourage children to think of multiple solutions, remind them to listen to one another's ideas, suggest additional solutions by prompting
TRY a solution and see how it works for everyone	Guide children in choosing a solution (let children decide as long as it is reasonable), provide support in carrying out and evaluating the solution

Think about this…

How do you tend to approach disagreements or conflicts with other adults—do you take charge, go along with the opinions of others, try to smooth over angry feelings, focus on solutions, etc.?

Do you find compromising with others to be easy or challenging? Are there particular areas or situations in which it is more difficult for you to compromise?

Try this today…

When reading stories or discussing events that have happened (e.g., a story that a child is sharing with the class) that involve a conflict or difference of opinion, take opportunities to ask children to think of as many possible solutions to the problem as they can. Guide children in thinking about the consequences of these possibilities for each person involved (e.g., *If they decided to play restaurant in the loft, most of the kids would be happy, but what about the child who is afraid to climb up to the loft? What would he do?*).

Solving Problems

4.2

READ AND DISCUSS: *DECIDING TOGETHER*

Children listen to the story and discuss the importance of listening to everyone's ideas and working together to THINK of solutions to TRY that will make everyone feel okay.

Before Reading

Have you and a friend ever had to figure out a problem together, like how to share something that you both wanted? How did you decide what to do?

In this story, the kids help Z learn that it's fair to decide things together. That means that everyone gets to share their ideas and everyone listens to each other. Then you can think and decide together on a fair solution that works for everyone.

As you listen to the story, pay attention to the different ideas that Z and the kids have for how to solve their problem, and whether they think of a fair solution.

During Reading

After Z and the kids found the caterpillar in the tree house, what was the problem that they had? *(They wanted to do different things with the caterpillar)* What were some of the different ideas they had about how to solve their problem? *(Put the caterpillar in the garden, smoosh it, take it home, keep it in the tree house)*

Would it have been fair for Z to be the only one to decide what to do with the caterpillar? How would the other kids have felt if they just had to do it Z's way? *(Sad, angry, like Z wasn't listening to them)*

After Z and the kids thought of different solutions for what to do with the caterpillar, which solution did the kids decide to try? *(Kayla was going to bring her bug house to the tree house)* Was this a fair solution? Why? *(Everyone decided together, everyone felt okay about it)*

After Reading

Do you think it is fair if only one person gets to decide how to solve a problem? What can make it hard to be fair? *(People want things to be their way, forget to think about or ask about others' feelings and ideas, feel too upset about the situation to listen to others' ideas, can't think of other solutions)*

What could you do if someone you were playing with wanted things to be just their way? *(Say how you feel, suggest other ideas, ask an adult to help you work it out)*

Extension: You may wish to brainstorm what children would do if they found a caterpillar at school, highlighting the many solutions.

Solving Problems

4.2

EXPLORE AND PRACTICE: FIND A SOLUTION

Children discuss the last two steps in solving problems (Think, Try), practice generating solutions to problems presented in scenarios, and then problem-solve with a peer during collaborative play.

Set the Stage

Review the first two steps in solving a problem and introduce the last two steps, referring to the *Problem-Solving* poster.

[STOP, TALK] When you have a problem, the first thing to do is to stop and calm down, and then to talk to one another so that you can figure out the problem.

[THINK] Once you have figured out the problem, the next step is to think about what you could do to solve the problem. There can be many different ways to solve a problem, so it is important to listen to everyone's ideas so that you can decide together in a fair way.

[TRY] After you have thought of some different ways to solve the problem, the last step is to choose one and try it out. You can ask yourself three questions to decide what would be a good solution to try. You can ask: *Is it safe? Is it fair? Will everyone feel okay?*

Guide children in discussing 1-2 conflict scenarios, reminding them that there can be many ways to solve a problem. For each scenario:
- State the problem in words.
- Discuss 2-4 possible solutions (including poor solutions).
- Predict the consequences of 1-2 of these solutions for each of the characters to determine if the solution could be a good one.

Suggested Scenarios
- *You and a friend both want to ride bikes on the playground, but there is only one bike left.*
- *You are trying to build a sandcastle, but other kids keep running back and forth through the sandbox.*
- *You are drawing a picture when someone else asks to use the crayons, but you want to keep using them.*

Extension: Have children share problem-solving ideas with their buddies before inviting a few to share with the class.

Solving Problems

4.2

Facilitate the Activity

Set out the Buddy Buckets and explain that children will now be able to practice being good problem-solvers as they play with their buddy (designate a length of time that they will play). Invite buddies to choose a container, and provide support to them as they choose a bucket and decide fairly how to play together. As children play together, provide support and positive reinforcement for any problem-solving efforts, repeating the relevant steps (*You and your buddy had a problem because there was only one dinosaur and you both wanted to play with it. You came up with a good solution to take turns with the dinosaur!*). When necessary, remind children that if the solution they try doesn't work for everyone, they can think of some more ways to solve the problem and try another one, and guide them in doing so.

Wrap It Up

Did you and your buddy have different ideas about what to play? How did you solve the problem and decide together? *(Thought of solutions, picked one to try)*

How do you know if the solution you decide to try is a good one? *(It is fair, everyone feels okay about it)*

SUPPLEMENTAL ACTIVITIES

Joint Committees: Consider giving small groups of children a role in decision-making about classroom activities and routines. Small groups are a manageable context in which you can provide support as children practice sharing ideas, listening, negotiating, and compromising. For example, choose 3 children each day to select the afternoon story or song together. Facilitate this discussion so that children can all participate in the decision.

Problem-Solving Role Play: Discuss problem-solving scenarios. Invite children to think of a fair solution and to role play an ending to the scenario.

Cooperating

4.3 PreK

OVERVIEW

Read and Discuss: *Being a Team*

Explore and Practice: Teamwork in Action – Block Construction

MATERIALS

- *Being a Team* storybook
- Blocks or building materials
- *Cooperation* cards

GOALS

This set of activities is designed to:
- Foster collaborative teamwork skills.
- Promote fairness in playing and working together.

LEARNING OBJECTIVES

Children will be able to:
- Name ways to cooperate with others.
- Practice cooperating with peers in a shared activity.

KEY CONCEPTS AND VOCABULARY

When you work together with someone else, you can think of new ideas and do things that you can't do alone.

Cooperation means that you listen to each other's ideas, share, and help one another.

Cooperating

4.3   PreK

RESEARCH AND RELEVANCE

As children develop their abilities to express their feelings and ideas, to understand the feelings and perspectives of others, and to exhibit self-control by paying attention and inhibiting impulsive behavior, they are better equipped to play with partners or small groups of children and to cooperate with others. Cooperative play creates opportunities for children to teach and learn from one another—two (or more) heads are often better than one! It also motivates children to be aware and supportive of mutual group goals, fosters a sense of interdependence, and emphasizes that communication and teamwork are important for success—each person's contributions are important and valued.

Think about this...

Do you tend to prefer to work alone or with others? Does that differ at home compared to at work? What do you find challenging and/or helpful about working alone or together?

How often do you plan activities in which the children in your class can work with a partner or small group? What do you find challenging and/or helpful about facilitating group work with children?

Have you considered how you might use the physical space in your classroom to promote teamwork? Are areas and materials set up that bring children into close proximity and encourage cooperation? What changes could you make to achieve those goals, while maintaining necessary classroom structures?

Try this today...

Promote cooperation, turn-taking, and teamwork by setting up small group activities and centers with limited materials. For example, if four children are making collages at the art center, provide only 1 or 2 bottles of glue, or have pairs of children work together on one larger sheet of paper. Be mindful of children's individual developmental levels and their capacity to adapt to this challenge without creating extensive conflict, and be prepared to provide additional support for children's waiting, asking, and sharing with one another. Notice and specifically acknowledge children's cooperative behaviors.

> *I see that you have figured out how to share the stickers with one another—choosing one sticker and then passing them to the next person is a great idea to make sure that everyone gets to use them!*

sanfordharmonyprogram.org   ©Arizona State University All Rights Reserved

Cooperating

4.3 PreK

READ AND DISCUSS: *BEING A TEAM*

Children listen to the story and discuss why it can be helpful to work together rather than alone, and how to do so fairly and cooperatively.

Before Reading

What is something that you like to play with other people? When you play or work with other people, what are some things you do to make sure that you are working as a team?

In this story, the kids help Z learn that it is important to *cooperate* with others and work as a team. That means that everyone listens to each other and shares and helps one another. Cooperating can make working together much more fun for everyone!

As you listen to the story, pay attention for times when Z and the kids are *not* cooperating and other times when they are working as a team.

During Reading

What happened when Gabriel and Annie first tried to work together with Z to build the Zanderloo tower? *(Z didn't include them, Z didn't listen to them, Z didn't share the blocks)* Why did Z do that? *(Z was excited to play, wanted to show them the tower, forgot to share)*

How do you think Annie and Gabriel felt when they weren't able to work as a team with Z? *(Sad, disappointed, bored)*

Why is it important for everyone to get to work on what you're doing together? *(It's fair, everyone gets to play, everyone might have good ideas)*

What did Z, Gabriel, and Annie do to be fair and cooperate at the end of the story? *(Listened to each other's ideas, decided what to build together, helped each other, shared the blocks, worked on the tower together)*

Tip: Be sensitive to family and cultural differences in the emphasis placed on independence versus interdependence, while highlighting the positive aspects of cooperation and teamwork.

After Reading

When do you cooperate and work together with your classmates here at school? *(Play games together, clean up together, build things together)*

What are some things that you should do to be fair and cooperate when you are working together? *(Listen to each other's ideas and decide what to do together, share, take turns, help each other)*

Tip: Display the *Cooperation* cards as children share corresponding ideas.

Cooperating

4.3 PreK

EXPLORE AND PRACTICE: TEAMWORK IN ACTION – BLOCK CONSTRUCTION

Children work together on a collaborative construction activity.

Set the Stage

Show the class a bucket of blocks and ask them to brainstorm what they could build with them.

Explain that children will be working as teams to build something together, referring to the ways to show cooperation depicted on the *Cooperation* cards.

Everyone is going to get a chance to practice <u>cooperating</u> with one another while you work in teams to build something together with blocks. First, you will need to listen to each other's ideas so you can decide together what you're going to build. Then, remember to be fair and cooperate by sharing and taking turns and helping one another while you work. And because you're a team, it's important that each person on the team gets to work on what you build together.

Tip: If supplies are limited, or for additional monitoring, have teams take turns working at a "team center."

Facilitate the Activity

Divide children into teams (2-4 children each) and distribute building materials. As children work together, provide support and positive reinforcement for their cooperative efforts (*I can see your team <u>cooperating</u> by taking turns stacking blocks on your tower!*). If children are working separately or some are not participating, guide teams in collaborating (*It looks like you are building both a hospital and an airport. How will people at the airport get to the hospital? Good idea for <u>cooperating</u>—you could build a road together to connect them!*).

After teams have worked on their constructions, gather the class back together to discuss the experience.

Tip: Take photos of each team in action.

Wrap It Up

Did you have different ideas about what to build? How did you decide together? *(Listened to everyone's ideas, asked each other what to build)*

What are some ways that you cooperated with your team? *(Shared the blocks, took turns stacking blocks, handed each other blocks)*

Extension: Have children draw and dictate how they cooperated and worked together as a team, and create a display or class book with the reflections and team photos.

Cooperating

4.3

SUPPLEMENTAL ACTIVITIES

Team Projects: Occasionally throughout the year, set up activities that foster teamwork among the entire class or small groups of children. Breaking up some projects into smaller tasks assigned to "committees" can support teamwork practice in more manageable groups. Team projects might include:
- Gather large boxes, recyclables, or building materials and encourage children to decide as a group what to create together.
- Planning and preparing a simple meal.
- Choosing and developing a special activity or display for a Family Night.

Help

Being Considerate

4.4 PreK

OVERVIEW

Read and Discuss: *Z Gets the Ziggles*

Explore and Practice: Turn It Up, Turn It Down Song

MATERIALS
- *Z Gets the Ziggles* storybook

GOALS

This set of activities is designed to:
- Promote awareness that everyone has different preferences and behavioral styles.
- Promote consideration of the impact of one's behaviors on others.
- Foster self-regulation.

LEARNING OBJECTIVES

Children will be able to:
- Name and demonstrate ways to calm down.
- Practice intentionally changing their activity level in a movement game.

KEY CONCEPTS AND VOCABULARY

Everyone is unique in how they feel and how they do things.

Being *considerate* means showing that you care about other people's feelings.

It is important to make sure that what you are doing is *considerate* of the other people around you.

To calm down, you can:
- Take deep, slow breaths.
- Quiet your voice.
- Let your body relax.

Being Considerate

4.4 PreK

RESEARCH AND RELEVANCE

Every child has a unique temperament, with differences in the ways that they experience and express emotions, their preferred activity level, and their ability to self-regulate their attention, emotions, and behaviors. Because children all have unique sets of characteristics, sometimes they might experience their classmates as too noisy, active, or over-stimulating. Other children might find peers too quiet, passive, or even boring. It is in these situations when it is helpful to guide children in figuring out compatible ways to play together, while still supporting their expressions of individuality. It is important for children to notice when their behaviors are making it difficult for others to play with them and to adjust what they are doing or where they are doing it. It is also important for kids to know that it's okay to respectfully let others know when their behavior is too much for them to handle. Even when children are different in some ways, they can be supported in finding enjoyable ways to play and learn together.

Think about this…

How would you characterize your own behavioral tendencies in areas such as "talkativeness" or activity level? How quickly or slowly are you able to change these tendencies in a given situation?

What strategies do you find effective in working with adults or children whose communication or behavioral styles differ from your own?

Try this today…

Support children in their daily efforts at self-regulation. Some children may need extra facilitation, reminders, or an intentionally-planned space or activity that will reduce other demands and distractions so that they can better focus on controlling and adapting their behavior when appropriate. Establishing and using classroom signals (e.g., palms facing up/down to indicate "turn it up" or "turn it down") can be helpful in providing children with gentle reminders to adjust their behavior, without interrupting their activities. Be alert for when children seem overwhelmed and will require your assistance in calming down.

Being Considerate

4.4 PreK

READ AND DISCUSS: *Z GETS THE ZIGGLES*

Children listen to the story and discuss how it is okay to do things differently, but that it is important to be considerate of others around you.

Before Reading

What is something that makes you feel really excited or loud or wiggly? Have you ever been around someone else who was very excited or loud or wiggly, when you weren't feeling that way? What was that like?

Sometimes when people are having fun or feeling silly, they might get really excited, or really loud, or really wiggly. That can be fun, but sometimes it's *too much*! It can make it hard for the people around them to play. In this story, the kids help Z learn that it is important to be *considerate* and show that you care about other people's feelings. When what someone else is doing is *too much*, they can calm themselves down and relax so that everyone can play.

As you listen to the story, pay attention for what Z does to calm down when what Z is doing starts to become TOO MUCH for the kids.

During Reading

What were some things that Z did when Z had the ziggles? *(Made a lot of noise, bounced and boinged around, wouldn't stop moving)*

How did Z's ziggles affect the kids in the tree house? *(They couldn't hear each other, things got knocked over, they couldn't play)*

Do you think Z was making things hard for the kids on purpose? *(No)* Why was Z acting ziggly? *(Z was excited, didn't know how to calm down)*

What did the kids teach Z to do to calm down, so that they could all play together? *(Take deep breaths in and out, quiet Z's voice, relax Z's body)*

After Reading

Why is it important to pay attention to the people around you and make sure that you are not making things hard for them? *(So they can play and learn, so you are being considerate)*

Being Considerate

4.4 PreK

Let's practice calming down just like Z. Take a big, deep breath and then let it out slowly. Keep your voices quiet and let your body get very loose and soft. How does that feel? *(Relaxed, calm, quiet)*

What could you do if you are really excited and are having trouble calming down? *(Ask for help from an adult, take a break)*

Extension: Model and have children practice:
- Asking/signaling you or another adult for help in calming down.
- "Taking a break" (Have an established space in the classroom that is quiet and safe).

EXPLORE AND PRACTICE: TURN IT UP, TURN IT DOWN

Children practice changing the speed of their movements by "turning it up" and "turning it down" during a song.

Set the Stage

Ask the class how someone might be acting when they are feeling excited and ziggly inside *(Jumping up and down, running around, being loud)*.

Explain that it is okay to be excited, but it is important to be considerate of how others feel and to calm down when necessary.

Sometimes people feel excited and jumpy, and sometimes they feel quiet and still. It's okay that everyone can act in different ways, but you have to make sure that you are being *considerate* of how other people feel. If what you're doing is TOO MUCH and is making things hard for someone else, you can change what you are doing by "turning it up" or "turning it down" so that everyone can play.

Facilitate the Activity

Explain that children will practice by "turning it up" and "turning it down" during a song.

Have children face their buddies. Sing several rounds of *"If You're Happy and You Know It"*, varying the pace and intensity of the singing and movements. Begin with slow singing and small movements (e.g., *blink your eyes at each other, wiggle your fingers at each other*), and gradually speed up the song and use larger movements (e.g., *jump up and down, wiggle like fish*). Next, slow the song and movements down again. End the song with a quiet, calming voice and slow movement (e.g., *sit down quietly*).

Tip: At the transitions, cue children that it is time to "turn it up" or "turn it down."

sanfordharmonyprogram.org ©Arizona State University All Rights Reserved

Being Considerate

4.4 PreK

Wrap It Up

How did it feel when you were wiggling like a fish during the song? *(Excited, jumpy inside, out of breath)*

What did you do with your body so that you could "turn it down" and sit down quietly at the end of the song? *(Slowed down, took some deep breaths, looked at the teacher)*

What could you do if someone else around you is doing something that feels like TOO MUCH to you? *(Tell them what is making things hard for you, nicely ask them to change what they are doing, ask an adult for help)*

Extension: Model and have children practice stating how they feel and asking a peer to adjust behavior that is "too much" (e.g., *The noise is making it hard for me to look at my book. Could you please play more quietly?*).

SUPPLEMENTAL ACTIVITIES

Bubbles: Have children alternately pop bubbles with movements that are large (e.g., clap between hands, stomp) or small (e.g., poke, flick). Next, blow bubbles and have children walk through them *without* popping them.

Calming Down Book: Have children think about a time when they might need to "turn it down" at school (e.g., after coming in from the playground), and have them draw/dictate what they can do at that time or how they look when they are calm. Create a class book and keep in it the quiet area that has been established for "taking a break".

Fast/Slow and Loud/Quiet Counting: Establish a counting pattern (e.g., say 1-5 slowly and then say 6-10 quickly, then reverse the pattern) and have children practice adjusting their speed or volume of speaking as they count.

Fast and Slow Movement: Have children alternately do jumping jacks, hula hoop, march, etc. quickly and then slowly according to the speed of your counting. After practice, have buddies do this activity with a partner and have the buddy adjust the counting rate.

 # Peer Relationships

Unit 5

Peer Relationships

5.0

OVERVIEW

Unit 5 focuses on promoting attitudes and behaviors that are critical for maintaining positive and supportive peer relationships. Unit 5 also provides a review of children's experiences and learning throughout the year and creates an opportunity for connection with future growth.

GOALS

This unit is designed to help children:
- Develop a caring, pro-social orientation.
- Learn inclusive attitudes and behaviors.
- Take responsibility for their actions and make amends.
- Develop a forgiving attitude.
- Review areas of individual and group growth and change.
- Gain a sense of closure regarding their experiences together this year.

ACTIVITIES

5.1 Caring for Others
Children discuss the importance of being caring toward others, and then practice giving compliments and doing something kind for a peer.

5.2 Being Inclusive
Children discuss the importance of making sure that everyone feels welcomed and included, and practice inviting and including one another in a musical game.

5.3 Making Amends and Forgiving
Children discuss the idea that everyone makes mistakes and the elements of making amends.

5.4 Reflecting and Connecting
Children discuss feelings and memories at the end of the school year, and create a display of their favorite class memories.

Home-School Connections — Unit 5 PreK

5.1 Caring for Others

Suggested information to share with families in the classroom newsletter:

Our class is discussing the many ways that we can show caring toward others, and how doing and saying kind things can make both us and others feel good.

You may wish to:

- Ask your child about ways that they have helped a classmate "have a good day".
- "Catch" your child being kind to someone and point out how good that must have made the person feel.
- Model small acts of kindness during your daily activities and talk with your child specifically about how and why the act may have benefited the person.
- Brainstorm ways that your family could do kind things for others in your neighborhood or communities, or participate in a community service project as a family.

5.2 Being Inclusive

Suggested information to share with families in the classroom newsletter:

Our class is talking about the many ways that we can include others when we play and make sure that no one feels left out.

You may wish to:

- Ask your child about a time when someone invited them to play, and how that made them feel.
- Ask your child if they invited anyone to play with them this week, and what they did together.

Home-School Connections — Unit 5

5.3 Apologizing and Forgiving

Suggested information to share with families in the classroom newsletter:

Our class is talking about how sometimes even friends make mistakes, don't get along, or hurt one another's feelings. We are learning how it can be helpful to be a *fast forgiver*, and we are talking about ways that you can make an *apology in action* (*Say your part ~ Speak from the heart ~ Fix what's been broken apart*) when you have hurt someone or made a mistake.

You may wish to:

- Ask your child how they make an *apology in action.*
- Help your child think about how to "fix what's been broken apart"—how to take action in making things better with a family member or friend when your child has been hurtful to them in some way (e.g., give a hug, draw a picture or write a note to them, do something kind for them, fix something they have ruined).

5.4 Reflecting and Connecting

Suggested information to share with families in the classroom newsletter:

Our class is taking some time to remember special times and events in the past year, to reflect on how everyone has grown as an individual and as a classroom community, and to create some hopes and goals for the future.

You may wish to:

- Ask your child to share with you some of their favorite memories:
- Something they accomplished that makes them proud
- Something they learned from their classmates
- Something they helped their classmates learn
- Their favorite part of the day at school this year
- Something that happened at school this year that they will never forget
- Friendships they would like to continue

Caring for Others

5.1 PreK

OVERVIEW

Read and Discuss: *Have a Good Day*

Explore and Practice: Brighten Someone's Day

GOALS

This set of activities is designed to:
- Promote a caring, prosocial orientation toward others.
- Foster gratitude for others' kindnesses.

LEARNING OBJECTIVES

Children will be able to:
- Name ways to show kindness to others.
- Practice giving compliments and receiving compliments with gratitude.

KEY CONCEPTS AND VOCABULARY

Being kind and caring makes both you and others feel good.

You can show caring toward others by:
- Helping
- Sharing
- Saying kind things

Gratitude means appreciation or thankfulness.

Showing gratitude when others are kind to us makes them feel good.

A *compliment* is something kind that you say about someone else.

MATERIALS

- *Have a Good Day* storybook
- "Sunshine Stick" (cut out and attach sun to a popsicle stick)
- Paper, writing materials, and/or craft supplies

Caring for Others

5.1

RESEARCH AND RELEVANCE

Prosocial behaviors are those intended to benefit others, such as helping, comforting, saying kind things, and sharing. These behaviors are motivated by a desire to care for others rather than to please someone or to earn a reward. Children who have sensitive and nurturing adults in their lives learn what it is like to have caring, respectful, and compassionate relationships with others. Feeling valued, responded to, and cared for themselves helps children develop caring and empathy for others. In addition, when children feel connected to others—whether in close relationships and friendships or as being part of a community in which they feel acceptance and belonging—they develop concern for others and a sense of social responsibility toward them. Fostering children's prosociality in a group setting can promote a positive and caring emotional climate within the whole classroom.

Think about this…

How easy or challenging is it for you to think about and find time to intentionally do kind things for others? Do you tend to do so spontaneously, or in response to a need or request?

Is it easier to do kind things for some people rather than for others? What are some things that can make it difficult?

How easy or challenging is it for you to show gratitude when others do kind things for you or give you compliments?

Try this today…

Rather than exclusively focusing on children's prosocial actions (e.g., *That was really nice sharing!*), reinforce the child's prosocial disposition (e.g., *You are really someone who likes to help others!*) or focus on the positive consequences of their actions (e.g., *When you gave Tina a turn on the swing, it made her really happy.*). When appropriate, invite the other child to share their feelings (e.g., *Jason, I noticed that Lilia shared her stickers with you. Why don't you tell Lilia how that made you feel?*).

Caring for Others

5.1 — PreK

READ AND DISCUSS: *HAVE A GOOD DAY*

Children listen to the story and discuss ways to be kind to others and how doing so can make everyone feel good.

Before Reading

What is something kind that a friend has done for you? How did that make you feel?

In this story, the kids help Z learn that there are many ways to be kind and help someone else have a good day. Showing kindness and caring toward others can make them feel special, and can make you feel good too.

As you listen to the story, pay attention to the kind things that Z and the kids do for one another.

During Reading

What were some of the ways that Z was kind and caring toward Jordan and Mia? *(Z cleaned up, made them pictures, shared muffins)* How did those things make the kids feel? *(Special, happy, important, like Z cared about them)*

Having gratitude means showing that you are thankful to someone who has been kind to you. What did the kids say to Z to show their gratitude? *(Thank you)*

How did doing kind things for the kids make Z feel? *(Happy, good inside)* Why do you think it makes you feel happy when you do kind things for others? *(You see them happy, you know that you helped someone)*

Extension: Have children turn to their buddies and practice saying *thank you*.

After Reading

What are some ways that you can be kind to your classmates and help everyone have a good day? *(Share your things, say nice things to each other, help someone who is having trouble, give someone a compliment, show affection with a hug or high-five, smile at each other)*

When someone does something caring toward you or says something nice to you, what could you do or say to show gratitude to them? *(Say thank you, tell them how it made you feel, give them a hug)*

Caring for Others

5.1 PreK

EXPLORE AND PRACTICE: BRIGHTEN SOMEONE'S DAY

Children pass around a "Sunshine Stick" to practice giving and receiving compliments from their classmates, and then make a card for their buddy.

Set the Stage

Say something kind about the class (e.g., *I love how everyone in our class helps to put away the blankets so quickly at the end of our quiet time every afternoon!*) and explain that this was a compliment.

That was a *compliment* **about our class. A** *compliment* **is something kind that you say about someone else or about something they have done.**

Show the Sunshine Stick to the class.

This Sunshine Stick has a sun on it to show that when you are kind to someone, you can really brighten their day. We're going to use the Sunshine Stick to give our classmates *compliments* **and say kind things to one another.**

With a volunteer, model giving a compliment and showing gratitude when receiving a compliment (by saying *Thank you*). Emphasize that it makes people feel very special when you notice what kind of person they are or what they have done (rather than their appearance or belongings), giving a few examples (e.g., *I like how Keana always works hard to build really cool towers. Jared is a good friend because he shares with his classmates.*).

Give a compliment to the first child, and after they say *thank you*, hand them the stick. The child should turn and compliment the person next to them, who will say *thank you* and take the stick. Continue around the circle. After all children have had a turn, invite them to share how they felt when their classmate gave them a compliment (*Happy, special*).

Facilitate the Activity

Explain that children will be brightening their buddy's day by making Compliment Cards for them (have buddies sit together as they work). Invite children to dictate a compliment to write on their card. Encourage buddies to show gratitude toward one another after their card exchange.

Tip: If supplies are limited, or for additional monitoring, have buddies come to a "buddy center" in pairs to make cards.

Tip: To help children focus on others' positive traits and behaviors, prompt them to begin compliments with *"You are…"* or *"I like how you…"*.

Caring for Others

5.1 PreK

Wrap It Up

How did you feel when your buddy gave you a card? *(Happy, special, grateful)*

How does it help our class when people show kindness toward one another? *(Everyone has a good day, everyone feels happy, everyone cares about each other, we get along)*

Extension: Establish a permanent space with materials for children (or teachers) to create:

► Compliment cards.
► Thank you notes.

SUPPLEMENTAL ACTIVITIES

Buddy Bracelets: Set up a "buddy center" and invite children to come in pairs with their buddies to make beaded "buddy bracelets" for one another. Encourage children to show gratitude toward one another after their exchange. You may wish to establish a permanent space with materials for children (or teachers) to create bracelets, pictures, or "kindness cards" for their classmates, teachers, or family.

Classroom Caring Project: Discuss with children and choose an activity that the entire class can do together to show caring toward others (e.g., cleaning up an area on the shared school playground, making cards to give to patients in a local hospital). As you facilitate this project, emphasize how it will benefit others and how each child in the class is making a contribution.

Community Helpers: Invite someone from the community (e.g., a "community helper," a volunteer, a parent who helps a neighbor) to talk with children about the experience of helping others.

Sunshine Catchers: Encourage children to "catch" one another being kind. Make paper sun cutouts available so that children can write/dictate kind behaviors that they (or you) see their classmates doing. Create an ongoing classroom display with the suns and talk with children about how their kind acts benefit one another and the classroom community.

Z Sing-Along CD: Listen or dance to *Have a Good Day* and discuss how to help others have a good day.

Being Inclusive

5.2 PreK

OVERVIEW

Read and Discuss: *Including Everyone*

Explore and Practice: Everyone In

GOALS

This set of activities is designed to:
- Promote inclusive attitudes and behaviors.
- Foster empathy and kindness.

LEARNING OBJECTIVES

Children will be able to:
- Describe how it feels to be included and excluded.
- Practice inviting peers to join them in a game.

KEY CONCEPTS AND VOCABULARY

Including others means welcoming them and making sure that they can join in with everyone else.

It is important to find ways to make sure that everyone feels included.

MATERIALS
- *Including Everyone* storybook
- Music player

Being Inclusive

5.2 PreK

RESEARCH AND RELEVANCE

A positive classroom climate is supported when all children feel accepted and welcomed—by everyone. Unfortunately, there can be a number of reasons why children choose to explicitly or subtly exclude their peers:

- Situational constraints (e.g., *There's no more room at our table.*)
- Past peer behavior (e.g., *She's bossy when we play together.*)
- Peer abilities (e.g., *He doesn't know how to play the game we're playing.*)
- Peer group biases (e.g., *The jungle gym is only for the girls today!*)
- Peer pressure to exclude (e.g., *My other friends don't want to play with him.*)
- Circumstances unrelated to the peer (e.g., *I just need to talk to my other friend for a few minutes.*)
- Need to be alone or with just one or two peers (e.g., When children need to take a break or aren't ready to interact with multiple people)

No matter the reason, being excluded or feeling unwelcomed is hurtful. When children are guided in considering their reasons for exclusion (some of which may indeed be legitimate), they can then take ownership of their actions and become actively involved in finding a solution. Even though it is not always possible for *all* children to play or work together *all* of the time, helping children think about the perspective and feelings of the excluded child can motivate them to figure out alternatives that ensure that no one feels left out or unwelcomed.

Think about this…

As a child or an adult, have you ever been excluded from a group or activity? How did that make you feel?

Have you ever felt uncomfortable or unable to join in a conversation or activity with others? Is there something that someone else could have done to make it easier for you?

Try this today…

Promote and reinforce welcoming and inclusive play, and point out how good it makes others feel.

I heard you say hello to the new student in our class. I think that must have made him feel very welcome!

I saw that you added another car to your train today and invited some kids to be passengers—that must have been a lot of fun to play in a different way!

It looks like Alicia really appreciated that you made room for her to sit at the table with you.

Set clear classroom expectations about exclusion, and do not allow exclusion based on gender or any other social category.

It's not okay to say that only the girls can play in the loft this morning—the loft is for everyone. If there's not enough room in the loft right now for others to play, let's think together and figure out a way to make sure that everyone can have a turn.

Being Inclusive

5.2 PreK

READ AND DISCUSS: *INLCUDING EVERYONE*

Children listen to the story and discuss what it is like to be included and excluded, and how to figure out ways to make sure that everyone feels included.

Before Reading

How do you feel when someone invites you to play with them?

In this story, the kids help Z learn that it is kind to *include* others when you play. There are a lot of ways you can make sure that everyone feels included.

As you listen to the story, pay attention to how Z and the kids figure out ways to include others in a game.

During Reading

Why was Z going to find something else to do instead of playing Rumble Jumble? *(Z didn't know how to play)* What did the kids do to make sure that Z was included in the game? *(Let Z watch, taught Z how to play the game)*

Why did Z tell Jeremy that he couldn't play the game with them? *(Because there weren't enough pieces)* How do you think you would feel to be left out of something that others were doing? *(Sad, ignored, disappointed, lonely)*

How did Z and the kids include Jeremy? *(By playing with partners)* What would be another fair way to make sure that everyone got to play a game? *(Take turns watching and playing, get something to use as more pieces, play a different game)*

How do you think Jeremy felt when his friends figured out a way for him to join the game? *(Included, happy, like they cared about him)*

After Reading

Can it sometimes be okay to say *no* to someone who wants to play with you? When? *(When you want to play alone, when there isn't enough room at the table or area, when there aren't enough toys to share with another person)*

How could you say no kindly? *(Tell them why you can't play together, offer to play with them later, offer to take turns with the toys)*

If you want to play with someone and they tell you that you can't, what could you say or do? *(Ask them if they want to play later, ask someone else to play, ask an adult for help joining in)*

Tip: Emphasize that it is kind to include others when possible, and encourage children to ask an adult for help in figuring out how to do this (or how to say *no* kindly when it is not possible).

Being Inclusive

5.2 PreK

EXPLORE AND PRACTICE: EVERYONE IN

Children practice inviting classmates to join them in a musical game.

Set the Stage

Have children sit in a circle, emphasizing how everyone is included.

When you *include* others, it means that you welcome them and make sure they can join in with everyone else. Look around our circle. Is everyone in our class *included* in the circle?

Explain that children will be playing a musical game in which everyone gets to join in and be included.

Facilitate the Activity

Invite two children to stand in the middle to start the game. Point out which children are in the outside circle and which children are in the middle of the circle. Explain how to the play the game.

- When music is playing, everyone in the outside circle and in the middle of the circle can dance.
- When the music stops, everyone should freeze in place.
- Upon the teacher's instructions, each child in the middle of the circle can invite someone new into the middle (e.g., *Do you want to come into the circle with me?*).
- Everyone can dance when the music begins playing again.

Each time you stop the music, <u>give a different instruction</u> about whom to invite (e.g., *Invite someone who is wearing red…has a name that rhymes with "pack"…is standing next to the chalkboard.*). Tell children that it is okay if more than one person invites the same child into the middle of the circle. Continue playing until all children are in the middle of the circle. Then, give an instruction that allows you to be invited into the circle (e.g., *Invite the tallest person in the room.*).

At the end of the game, have children sit down in a circle to reflect on the experience.

Tip: Repeat the game as time allows, varying instructions so that different children have an opportunity to be invited into the middle of the circle earlier in the game.

Wrap It Up

How did you feel when you were invited into the middle of the circle? *(Happy, excited, included)*

How did it feel when you had to wait for a long time to come into the middle of the circle? *(Wanting to be included, left out)* When are times when you have to wait to be included? *(When kids are already playing together, when there aren't enough toys, when there isn't enough room)*

Tip: Point out that the kids who had to wait a longer time also had more classmates inviting them into the circle.

santordharmonyprogram.org ©Arizona State University All Rights Reserved

Being Inclusive

5.2 PreK

In this game, everyone got a chance to be included together in the middle of the circle. How did that make the game more fun? *(Everyone was included, everyone got to keep playing together, no one was left out)*

SUPPLEMENTAL ACTIVITIES

Jump In, Jump Out: Draw shapes on the ground with sidewalk chalk (or use hula hoops), one shape for each pair of buddies. Have buddies stand outside of a shape, and give different instructions for moving in and out of the shape:

- *Jump in on one foot, jump out on one foot*
- *Jump in and sit down, stand up and jump out*
- *Put two fingers in, take two fingers out*
- *Put your arms in and hold hands, let go and take your arms out*

Next, cross out half of the shapes and repeat the game, with two buddy pairs per shape. Repeat the game again with three or four buddy pairs per shape and then finally the whole class in one shape. When children realize that they have to change the game in order to include everyone, brainstorm solutions (e.g., draw a bigger shape, have buddy pairs take turns moving in and out of the same shape, etc...).

Let's Do Lunch: Designate a day for buddies to sit together and share a meal or snack, and have buddies create "invitations" to one another for this event. Build anticipation by having children help plan a special food, select music, or make festive decorations for the tables.

Making Amends and Forgiving

5.3 PreK

OVERVIEW

Read and Discuss: *Staying Friends*

Explore and Practice: Everyone Makes Mistakes

MATERIALS
- *Staying Friends* storybook

GOALS

This set of activities is designed to:
- Promote an awareness of the need to take responsibility for one's actions.
- Foster motivation and skills for making sincere and reparative amends.
- Promote a forgiving attitude toward others.

LEARNING OBJECTIVES

Children will be able to:
- Acknowledge that everyone makes mistakes.
- Describe and demonstrate ways to make amends in various scenarios.

KEY CONCEPTS AND VOCABULARY

Friends may get upset at each other sometimes but can still stay friends.

When you *make amends*, you:
- Say your part.
- Speak from the heart.
- Fix what's been broken apart.

To *forgive* means to let go of your angry feelings at someone who has hurt you.

Being a fast forgiver can help everyone feel better and focus on making the situation better.

Making Amends and Forgiving

5.3 PreK

RESEARCH AND RELEVANCE

Children (and adults) often make mistakes and do things that are insensitive, careless, or misguided, and this can result in hurt feelings, broken belongings, and damaged relationships. Learning how to stay calm and take steps to repair these situations and to maintain good feelings toward one another are important relationship skills.

Making Amends

Meaningful amends are more than simply saying the words "I'm sorry" (and it is not beneficial to force children to verbally apologize, especially when they aren't ready or don't recognize the harm that their actions have caused). Sincere amends are heartfelt and involve showing concern for the hurt person, taking responsibility for one's role in what happened, and trying to make restitution for the harm that was caused. Even when the offense was accidental, explaining one's part in what happened is important in clarifying the situation to the hurt person and can make them less likely to assume that others have hostile or aggressive intentions toward them. Making amends provides a way for children to show caring to someone they have hurt, which can also ease any guilt about their role in what happened.

Forgiving

Being able to forgive plays an important role in maintaining positive relationships. Forgiveness does not mean deciding that what the other person did is okay and forgotten. Forgiveness is a change (for the better) in the way that one thinks and feels about the person who has hurt or harmed them, and involves a number of complex skills, including emotional regulation, perspective-taking, and empathy. Being able to forgive someone and "let go" of negative feelings toward them can help children to avoid aggressive tendencies and other negative social behaviors and to maintain their relationships in spite of the conflicts that will inevitably occur.

Think about this...

When you are upset or in a conflict with someone, what strategies do you use to stay calm?

How easy or challenging is it for you to admit to others when you have made mistakes or poor choices, or when you have hurt someone?

Are you a "fast forgiver" or do you tend to stay angry or upset at others?

Try this today...

Be accepting of children's strong emotions—even negative ones—because everyone has a right to feel angry or upset or hurt on the inside. Providing caring support to children during these times and making it clear that it is not okay to act upon these feelings in unkind ways can help children remain calm, develop self-control, and become ready to forgive or make amends. Offer empathy and acceptance (rather than confrontation) when children make mistakes, while encouraging concern for others and responsibility for their actions.

Making Amends and Forgiving

5.3 PreK

READ AND DISCUSS: *STAYING FRIENDS*

Children listen to the story and discuss why it is important to show concern and take steps to make the situation better when you hurt someone, and why it is also important to be a fast forgiver.

Before Reading

An *accident* is something that someone doesn't do on purpose. Have you ever done something by accident that made someone else upset or hurt their feelings? What happened? What did you do to make things better?

In this story, Z and the kids accidentally hurt one another's feelings. The kids help Z learn that even when that happens, you can still figure out how to make things better and stay friends.

As you listen to the story, pay attention for times when Z and the kids feel hurt by something that the other has done, and what they do so that they are able to stay friends.

During Reading

How did Z feel to see the kids making the birdhouse without Z? *(Disappointed, sad, upset, angry, hurt)*

What did Z say? *(Z said that the birdhouse was silly, that they couldn't be friends anymore)* How do you think that made the kids feel? *(Sad, hurt, disappointed)*

Do you think that the kids left Z out and hurt Z's feelings on purpose or by accident? *(By accident, they didn't mean it)* If they didn't mean to hurt Z's feelings, why do you think they told Z their part in what happened and said they were sorry that Z was sad? *(They wanted Z to know what happened, they wanted Z to feel better, they wanted to show that they cared about Z, they wanted to still be friends)*

To forgive someone means that you let go of your angry feelings toward them. When you forgive someone, it doesn't mean that what they did was okay, but you stop being angry at them. Did Z forgive the kids? How did that make Z feel? *(Z felt better, stopped being angry)*

What did the kids do to make things better with Z? *(Talked about what happened, showed that they cared about Z's sad feelings, asked Z to help them hang the birdhouse)*

Tip: Remind children of classroom guidelines for expressing angry feelings *(e.g., It is okay to be angry and talk about it, but it isn't okay to hurt people or property)*.

Making Amends and Forgiving

5.3 PreK

After Reading

Why is it important to say what happened and show someone that you care when you hurt their feelings, even if you didn't do it on purpose? *(So they know what happened, so they feel better, to show that you care about them)*

Have you ever felt really upset at a friend? What can you do when that happens so that you don't say things that aren't kind? *(Try a calming down activity, take a break from playing with each other, tell them how you feel, talk about what happened, ask an adult for help)*

Why is it important to be a fast forgiver? *(You start feeling better, sometimes it is hard to think of what to do next when you are angry, the person that has hurt you can start feeling better)*

> **Extension:** Have children turn to their buddies and practice saying the words, "I forgive you."

EXPLORE AND PRACTICE: EVERYONE MAKES MISTAKES

Children discuss the idea that everyone makes mistakes and the elements of making amends.

Set the Stage

Make a series of silly or exaggerated mistakes (e.g., drop something, say a big word incorrectly, bump something over, forget to do something) and each time, label your action as a "mistake" (e.g., *Oops! I made a mistake and forgot that we were going to sit outside today!*).

Facilitate the Activity

Discuss the idea that everyone makes mistakes.

What does it mean to make a mistake? *(To do something that isn't right, to do something the wrong way)*

Sometimes people make mistakes, and those mistakes can hurt others' feelings or ruin their belongings. Let's think about some mistakes that people might make. Do you think that kids ever use things that belong to someone else? Give a thumbs up if you think that kids sometimes make that mistake, and a thumbs down if kids never make that mistake.

Making Amends and Forgiving

5.3 PreK

Continue discussing several examples of common mistakes (e.g., *knock over what someone else is building, forget to take turns, say things that aren't nice to others*) and have the class decide whether children (and adults) ever make that mistake. You may wish to admit to making some of those mistakes yourself.

So it seems like there are a lot of mistakes that people can make. Do you think that everyone can make mistakes?

Discuss the importance of finding ways to continue having caring relationships even when mistakes occur, and introduce the idea of making amends.

Everyone can mistakes, and even when this happens by accident, it is important to *make amends* by talking about what happened and trying to make things better.

Explain each of the elements of making amends, demonstrate the corresponding signals with both hands and have the class copy your actions.

Say your part (point to your mouth)
To make an amends, you first *say your part*. That means that you stay calm and explain what happened, even if it was an accident. Being honest about what you did helps the other person understand what happened, and that can make them feel better.

So if you came around the corner and accidentally knocked over someone's tower of blocks, what could you say to your classmate to *say your part*? *(I didn't see your tower, I forgot to look where I was going, I was going too fast)*

Speak from the heart (cover your heart with your hands)
To *speak from the heart* means that you say something kind to let the other person know that you care about what happened. Even if it was an accident, it is important for the other person to know that you really care that they are sad or upset.

What could you say to *speak from the heart* to the person whose tower you ruined? *(I wish your tower wasn't ruined, I wish you weren't sad)*

Fix what's been broken apart (clasp hands as if putting something back together)
To *fix what's broken apart* means that you find a way to make things better. If something actually got broken or ruined, you might need to help fix it or clean it up. But it might be that someone's feelings that have gotten a little bit broken or hurt. Then you could *fix what's broken apart* by thinking of a way to make that person feel good again, like saying something nice or inviting them to play.

If you knocked over someone's tower, what could you do to *fix what's broken apart*? *(Help clean up the blocks, help build another tower, offer to share the tower you guild)*

Tip: If children begin sharing specific examples and naming peers (e.g., *One time Joey took my marker!*), redirect them to the general question (e.g., *Is this a mistake that kids can sometimes make? Thumbs up or down?*).

Tip: Even if children make a sincere amends, they may need time before they are ready to play together again. Establish a safe space for children to take a break when upset.

Making Amends and Forgiving 5.3

Wrap It Up

Let's use our words and hand signals to say the three parts of making an amends to someone. *(Say your part, Speak from the heart, Fix what's been broken apart)*

Why is it important to make amends when people are upset or hurt by something that you have done? *(So the person feels better, to show that you care, to make things better for them)*

What can you do if someone makes amends to you? *(Forgive them, listen to them)*

Tip: Emphasize that children can ask an adult if they need help in managing their emotions, finding the right words or thinking of ways to make the situation better, or responding to someone's amends.

SUPPLEMENTAL ACTIVITIES

Calming Down: Teach children a calming activity like taking deep breaths, counting slowly, or picturing something beautiful. Guide them in practicing this activity when they are physically aroused (e.g., after coming in from recess) and encourage them to try it when they are feeling upset at someone.

Making Amends Role Play: Discuss some conflict scenarios and invite children to role play the scenario and demonstrate making amends.

Reflecting and Connecting

5.4 PreK

OVERVIEW

Read and Discuss: *Remembering Friends*

Explore and Practice: Memory Masterpiece

MATERIALS

- *Remembering Friends* storybook
- Large butcher paper or construction paper and art supplies

GOALS

This set of activities is designed to:
- Provide a review of what children have learned and experienced throughout the year.
- Provide an opportunity for children to consider how they have grown and changed.
- Encourage thinking and planning for the future.

LEARNING OBJECTIVES

Children will be able to:
- Recall memories from the school year.
- Identify ways that they have changed and grown.
- Describe their feelings about the school year coming to an end.

KEY CONCEPTS AND VOCABULARY

This year we have learned more about:
- Ourselves
- Each other
- How to be a community

We have grown and changed in many ways.

We will keep learning and growing.

Reflecting and Connecting

5.4

RESEARCH AND RELEVANCE

The end of the school year can bring a mix of emotions as children (and adults) prepare to transition away from familiar routines and structures and to say goodbye to many of those with whom they have developed relationships across the year. Taking time at the end of the school year to reflect upon significant events, accomplishments, relationships, and growth can provide opportunities to:

- Feel a sense of belonging and connection as they remember shared experiences.
- Feel valued as they recognize their importance and contributions to the class.
- Feel a sense of pride as they celebrate the accomplishments of individuals and the class as a whole.
- Gain a deeper understanding of themselves as they consider how they have grown, learned, and changed.
- Take ownership of their learning and growth as they make plans for the future.

Think about this…

What is something that was particularly frustrating, challenging, or stressful in your work this year? What is something that you are proud of accomplishing with your class this year?

How have you grown professionally this year? How has this impacted your work this year, or how will it impact your work in the future?

What will you remember most about the group of children in your class this year? What is something that you hope they remember about *you* or about their experiences in your classroom this year?

Try this today…

Take time to share individually with each child in your classroom some specific messages about how you have seen them grow, what you will remember about them, or how they have made a positive impact on you, their classmates, or the classroom community.

Reflecting and Connecting

5.4

READ AND DISCUSS: *REMEMBERING FRIENDS*

Children listen to the story and discuss why it is important to remember time spent together and to think about how they have changed and grown.

Before Reading

What is something special that you remember about this school year?

In this story, Z and the kids think back on the time they have spent with one another and all of the memories that they have together.

As you listen to the story, pay attention to how the kids and Z feel as they remember their time together, and listen for what they hope will happen in the future.

During Reading

How did Kayla and Z remember feeling when they first met? *(Nervous and shy)* How did that change over time? *(No longer shy, became comfortable)*

What were some of the memories Z and the kids shared? *(Taking care of a caterpillar, blowing bubbles together, Z being ziggly)*

What are some of the things that the kids helped Z learn? *(How to get along, what they had in common, how to calm down)*

After Reading

How did you feel when you started school and met your classmates this year? *(Nervous, shy, excited, confused)*

How have your feelings stayed the same or changed since the beginning of the year? Why? *(Got to know classmates, learned and had fun, got used to classroom activities, learned where things are and what to do, made friends)*

Why is it nice to think about things that you did together with friends? *(Makes you happy, you remember the fun you had together, you see how you have changed since then)*

Tip: Have children share and compare their feelings with their buddy before sharing with the class.

sanfordharmonyprogram.org ©Arizona State University All Rights Reserved

Reflecting and Connecting

5.4 PreK

EXPLORE AND PRACTICE: MEMORY MASTERPIECE

Children discuss favorite memories from the school year and work cooperatively to create a representation of those memories.

Set the Stage

Display the long piece of blank butcher paper and explain that children will be creating a banner that represents some of the memories they share from their time together as a classroom community.

Today we are going to make a banner together that shows the things that we remember about being part of (class name). Remembering what we have done together helps us to see how we have all grown and changed this year. Everyone will work on it together because we have all been an important part of this class.

Invite children to share memories from the past school year, providing specific prompts as needed:

Who can remember a time when our class showed teamwork?
Can you remember a time when a classmate did something really nice for you?
What was your favorite thing to do on the playground with your friends?

Record the children's memories directly onto the banner.

Facilitate the Activity

Explain that the children will be working together on the "memory masterpiece" by adding paintings or drawings of their own favorite class memories to the banner. Have children sit with buddies or in small groups around the banner, and encourage them to share their memories with one another as they work.

Gather the class back together to reflect on the experience.

Tip: Take photos of children working together and add them to the display.

Wrap It Up

What are some memories that your classmates shared that you remember as well?

What are some ways that you are different now than you were earlier in the year?
(know how to____, have new friends, grew bigger)

How do you feel when you look at our memory masterpiece? *(Happy, included, sad to say goodbye)*

Reflecting and Connecting

5.4

SUPPLEMENTAL ACTIVITIES

Classmate Appreciation: For each classmate, have children dictate or write one kind word to describe them, writing these adjectives on a slip of paper that is placed into a personal "mailbox" for each child.

Cross-Grade Scramble Up: Arrange a day when children can spend a lunch or snack period with children from the next grade in school (e.g., buddy children with an older peer, or partner small groups of children with small groups of children from the older grade). Prior to the lunch, help children prepare by brainstorming as a class some things that they could talk about or would like to ask the older students (e.g., *What is the best part of being in your grade? What was the coolest thing you learned this year?*).

My Future Me: Guide children in discussing some ways that they think school will be different next year (e.g., *new classmates, different classroom, different books and activities*). Next, talk about ways that they themselves might be different next year (e.g., *will grow taller, will know more children at school, will learn how to count higher or write some words*), and discuss what they might do over the school break that will help make that change (e.g., *eat healthy, read books with family members, play with friends, try a new activity, etc.*). Have children draw and/or dictate how they imagine themselves to be different next year. You may wish to mail children's work to them at home prior to the beginning of the next school year.

Thinking Back, Thinking Ahead: Throughout the last weeks of school, take time to guide children in reflecting on memories of the past school year and hopes for the future.
- *What is something that you did this year that makes you proud?*
- *What will you miss most about being in our class?*
- *What is the nicest thing that a classmate did for you this year?*
- *What is one way that you have become a better friend or classmate this year?*
- **What is one thing that you hope doesn't change next year?**
- *What is one way that you want to help your classroom community next year?*
- *What is one thing that you think will be easier next year?*
- *What is something that you are looking forward to about next year?*